Dramasci

Beowulf

A play based on the Anglo-Saxon epic poem

David Calcutt

Text © David Calcutt 2001

Original illustrations © Nelson Thornes Ltd 2001

The right of David Calcutt to be identified as author of this work has been asserted by him in accordance with the Copyright, Designs and Patents Act 1988.

All rights reserved. No part of this publication may be reproduced or transmitted in any form or by any means, electronic or mechanical, including photocopy, recording or any information storage and retrieval system, without permission in writing from the publisher or under licence from the Copyright Licensing Agency Limited, of 90 Tottenham Court Road, London W1T 4LP.

Any person who commits any unauthorised act in relation to this publication may be liable to criminal prosecution and civil claims for damages.

Published in 2001 by:
Nelson Thornes Ltd
Delta Place
27 Bath Road
CHELTENHAM
GL53 7TH
United Kingdom

06 07 08 09 / 10 9 8 7 6 5 4

A catalogue record for this book is available from the British Library

ISBN 0-17-432656-4

Illustrations by Richard Johnson and Peters & Zabransky
Page make-up by Peter Nickol

Printed in Croatia by Zrinski

CONTENTS

Series Editor's Introduction   IV
Introduction   V
The Characters   VII

BEOWULF

Act I	Scene 1	1
	Scene 2	9
	Scene 3	18
	Scene 4	32
	Scene 5	48
Act II	Scene 1	52
	Scene 2	56
	Scene 3	63
	Scene 4	71

Looking back at the play   80

Series Editor's Introduction

Dramascripts is an exciting series of plays especially chosen for students in lower and middle years of secondary school. The titles range from the best in modern writing to adaptations of classic texts such as *A Christmas Carol* and *Silas Marner*.

Dramascripts can be read or acted purely for the enjoyment and stimulation that they provide; however, each play in the series also offers all the support that pupils need in working with the text in the classroom:

- **Introduction** – this offers important background information and explains something about the ways in which the play came to be written.
- **Script** – this is clearly set out in ways that make the play easy to handle in the classroom.
- **Notes** explain references that pupils might not understand, and language points that are not obvious.
- **Activities** – at the end of scenes, acts or sections – give pupils the opportunity to explore the play more fully. Types of activity include: discussion, writing, hot-seating, improvisation, acting, freeze-framing, story-boarding and artwork.
- **Looking back at the play** – this section has further activities for more extended work on the play as a whole, with emphasis on characters, plots, themes and language.

John O'Connor

Introduction:
Beowulf

The story of Beowulf has been with me for a long time. I first came across it when I was a boy, in a version for children in my local library. What gripped me most at the time were the illustrations of the monsters – Grendel, Grendel's Mother and the Dragon. They were black and white pen drawings, all swirling lines and shadows, and, to me, very frightening. I was a great believer in monsters then.

Monsters are central to *Beowulf* – three of the most terrifying monsters ever imagined. But it isn't just a story of the hero who kills them and brings an end to their reign of terror. If it was, it would have a happy ending, and it doesn't. The people for whom Beowulf kills the first two monsters – the Scyldings – are doomed to be destroyed in a blood-feud. And Beowulf himself, as an old man, dies fighting the last one, and with his death comes the end of his own people – the Geats – also destroyed in a blood-feud with another clan.

It seems that although Beowulf can save people from monsters, he can't save them from themselves. In this sense, then, the real

INTRODUCTION

danger doesn't come from outside – from the wild wastes where Grendel and his Mother live, or the cave that is the dwelling place of the Dragon – but it comes from inside, from human beings. And I think this is what the poem is really about, and why it still rings true today, a thousand years after it was first written down.

Those same rivalries and blood-feuds that lead to war and destruction are still very much with us. The monsters are still on the loose, wreaking havoc in the world, but we know now that those monsters are human. They're not outside, but within us. That's the thorny problem the original poem deals with: how to defeat those monstrous impulses and forces that live inside us and lead us, from time to time, to destroy each other.

The poem doesn't find a proper solution to the problem, and neither does this play. But it does contain glimpses of the possibility of an answer. Hrothgar's building of his Hall is one, though it is only temporary. And the faithfulness Beowulf shows to Hrothgar, and his own lord, Hygelac, and the faithfulness that Wiglaf shows to Beowulf in turn, is another. But again, only temporary. Perhaps that is the truth the poem contains, and that I hope is contained in this play: that all solutions are temporary, but that, even against all the odds, we must remain faithful to those people and things that we value.

David Calcutt

The Characters

The three Fates, or Norns:
URD
VEDANDI
SKULD

Scyldings:
CHORUS OF SCYLDINGS
HROTHGAR   King of the Scyldings
WEALTHEOW   Hrothgar's wife and queen
ASHERE   Scylding nobleman, Hrothgar's close friend
UNFERTH   Scylding nobleman
COASTGUARD

Geats:
CHORUS OF GEATS
BEOWULF   Geat warrior and hero, later their king
OLD BEOWULF
WIGLAF   Young Geat warrior
SLAVE

Creatures:
GRENDEL   a monster
GRENDEL'S MOTHER
THE DRAGON

The set is simple and sparse. On stage right is a single raised platform, just wide enough for one actor. At the rear centre is a representation of a large ash tree, with branches, trunk and roots revealed. A pool of water lies at the base of the tree. The ash tree is as described in the opening section.

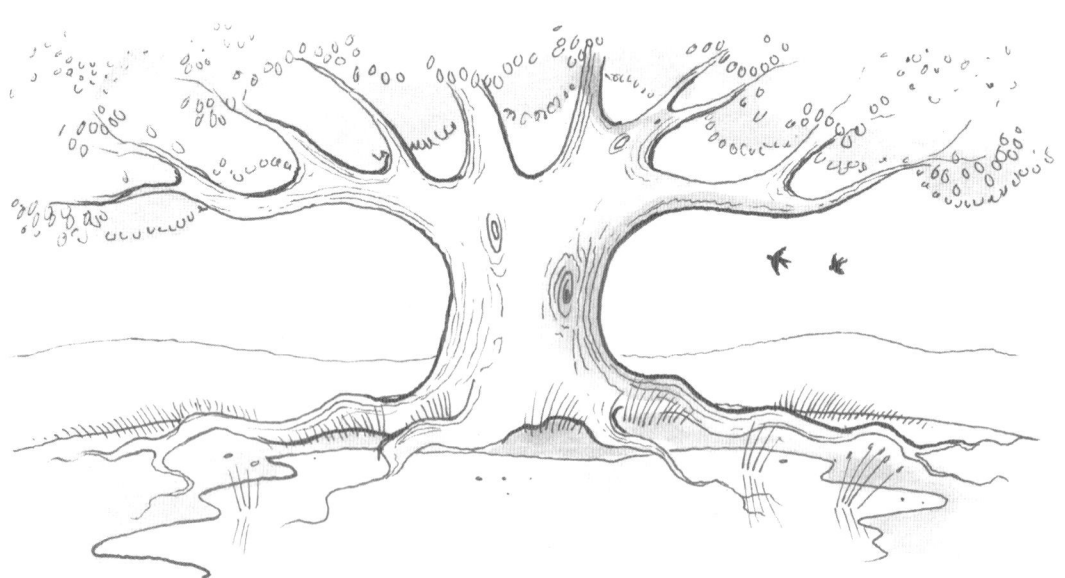

BEOWULF

ACT I

Scene 1 • Grendel comes to the Hall of Heorot

The three FATES, or Norns, enter. They are young women: URD, VEDANDI and SKULD. They speak as they enter, approaching the ash tree.

URD	Here grows a tree.	1
VEDANDI	A tree, whose roots are the heartbeat of the world.	
SKULD	An ash tree, holding the sky in its branches.	
URD	Yggdrasill, that always was.	
VEDANDI	Yggdrasill, that is, and will always be.	
SKULD	Yggdrasill, the world-tree.	
URD	There, in its branches, a hawk, an eagle.	
VEDANDI	There, circling its trunk, a red squirrel.	
SKULD	There, deer and goats eat its leaves and bark.	
URD	And coiled deep within its roots, a dragon…	10
VEDANDI	A dragon, gnawing the roots of the tree…	

 **Yggdrasill** *The description of Yggdrasill is taken from* The Prose Edda *by Snorri Sturluson. In Norse mythology, Yggdrasill was the centre of the world, and joined together the heavens, the earth, and the dark regions beneath the earth.*

ACT I SCENE 1

SKULD	A dragon that one day will devour the world.
URD	But not the tree. The tree will not die.
VEDANDI	The tree, Yggdrasill, cannot die.
SKULD	The tree, the world-tree, exists forever.
URD	And here beneath that tree we sit.
VEDANDI	Here is our home, by this pool.
SKULD	We sit here and gaze into the clear water.
URD	And see all that has happened.
VEDANDI	All that is happening.
SKULD	All that will ever happen.
URD	Future, present, past.
VEDANDI	All one, all now.
SKULD	A moment unfolding into eternity.
URD	A river that flows into its own source.
VEDANDI	A serpent encircling the whole earth…
SKULD	Endlessly eating its own tail.
URD	Here we sit and tell our tales.
VEDANDI	And each tale we tell is a life that's lived.
SKULD	The lives of men on middle-earth…
URD	Who step beneath the sun and breathe…
VEDANDI	Who carve the wind and cleave the waves…
SKULD	Who make their names within the world…
URD	Those whose minds are sharp as swords…
VEDANDI	Whose hearts are dark…
SKULD	Whose doom is death.

ACT I SCENE 1

Chorus of SCYLDINGS enter and speak to the audience. Their lines may be spoken individually, in small groups, or as one.

SCYLDINGS And the tale the Fates tell begins with us
The Scyldings, people of the North-lands
Our ancestor, Scyld, came here as an orphan
Abandoned, adrift in an open boat
He was cast up on the shore, he thrived and he prospered
Grew in might and power and became a great warrior
Subduing the land, he established his ownership
Claimed its kingship by right of conquest
And when his life's term ended he went back to the waves
A boat took his body to the sea's keeping
So the line was established, a glorious race
Lords and ring-givers, they rewarded their people
Fought hard battles, defeated their enemies
And our country grew rich, and we've grown rich with it
A proud tribe, fearsome and feared
The children of Scyld, masters of this land.

HROTHGAR enters and speaks to the SCYLDINGS.

HROTHGAR All that you say is true. What tribe of the north has earned more respect? Who is more feared in war? We all bear the scars of battles we've fought together. I, Hrothgar, your king, haven't shirked my responsibility there! But are we to be no more than warriors? Is war our only trade? The land's at peace. The days of fighting are over. When battles are done with, what comes next? I'll tell you. We'll build. Create something of beauty, here on this earth. A hall, such as no one has seen before, a great hall to house the bold spirits of the Scyldings. On the hilltop above the sea we'll build it, and the light from its windows will shine out like a beacon, so the glory of the Scyldings will be known across the world.

 **Scyld** *The name means shield. Scyld was the shield or protector of his people, who were named after him Scyldings, 'Scyld's People'.*

ACT I SCENE 1

HROTHGAR goes.

SCYLDINGS We do as he commands
Begin the hall's building   70
High on the hilltop
Erect walls and roofs
Windows wide
Beams inlaid with gold
A wide doorway
Wondrously carved
And above the doorway
A stag's antlers
Brought down by an arrow
A marvellous beast   80
So the hall takes its name
The Hall of the Stag
And a feast is held
There's meat and wine
The sound of the harp
The song of the poet
And the flame leaps high
Strikes the night with its spear
And the darkness unfolds
A bright blaze of glory   90
And for all time it burns
The praise of its people.

The SCYLDINGS turn and face away. The FATES speak softly, as if they are chanting a spell, conjuring Grendel with their voices.

URD The flame is out.

VEDANDI The dark descends.

 **The Hall of the Stag** *Heorot.*

4

ACT I SCENE 1

SKULD	Night thickens.	
URD	Silence.	
VEDANDI	Stillness.	
SKULD	Silence.	**100**
URD	The king and the queen have gone to their bed.	
VEDANDI	The warriors sleep in the dreaming hall.	
SKULD	The poet's song is locked in his skull.	
URD	Stillness.	
VEDANDI	Silence.	
SKULD	Stillness.	
URD	But listen.	
VEDANDI	Out there, in the darkness…	
SKULD	Something is stirring…	
URD	A movement…	**110**
VEDANDI	A shudder…	
SKULD	A shiver of fear.	
URD	A creature is crawling from the earth's deep…	
VEDANDI	Dragging itself up out of pool and fen…	
SKULD	As if from the very beginning of time.	
URD	It moves now over the frozen ground.	
VEDANDI	And every step is a scream of agony.	
SKULD	Each heavy footfall a howl of pain.	
URD	As it passes the grasses wither.	
VEDANDI	Creatures whimper in fear.	**120**
SKULD	Even the stars stare down in horror.	

ACT I SCENE 1

URD	And behind the dark face, two wicked eyes.	
VEDANDI	Behind the eyes, a wicked brain.	
SKULD	Lodged in the brain, dreams of bone and blood.	
URD	And hate.	
VEDANDI	Hate for the light.	
SKULD	Hate for the harp.	
URD	Hate for the laughter.	
VEDANDI	Hate for the song.	
SKULD	Hate for the hearts and the hopes of men.	130
URD	And dragging that lumber of pain…	
VEDANDI	Hauling that cumbersome weight of agony…	
SKULD	Bearing that burden of brutal hate…	
URD	The creature crosses the wild wastes of earth…	
VEDANDI	Slides its shadow between fence and gatepost…	
SKULD	And stands before the great doors of Heorot.	
	During the above, GRENDEL has appeared onstage – a massive, monstrous figure, part-human, part-beast. It should stand or hang centrally, above and dominating the stage. Now the SCYLDINGS turn and speak with urgency. Percussion or music of some kind may accompany their speech.	140
SCYLDINGS	And the doors burst wide Cracking Splintering They crash inwards The hall booms Roaring And we're up on our feet And there's something among us A black bolt from heaven	150

	A bellowing tempest	
	A thunderclap of hair and teeth	
	We strike with our swords	
	The blades shatter	
	Swing axe and club	
	They just bounce off	
	And we're caught in this storm of blood and ripped flesh	
	Sucked in by the whirlwind	
	Spinning	
	Falling	160
	Into the howling murderous centre	
	Limbs ripped	
	Bodies mangled	
	Chewed	
	Gulped	
	And nothing remains but the ravaged hall	
	And dark blood dripping from the ruined walls.	

The SCYLDINGS go. As the FATES speak, GRENDEL also disappears from the stage.

URD	So it begins.	170
VEDANDI	This tale of murder, bloodshed, horror.	
SKULD	It begins but does not end.	
URD	We who sit and tell the fates of men…	
VEDANDI	We who knot fast the bonds of their lives…	
SKULD	We shall not let it end.	
URD	It will go on.	
VEDANDI	Night after night.	
SKULD	Season after season.	
URD	The killing, the slaughter.	
VEDANDI	The beast coming out of the waste-land.	180

ACT I SCENE 1

SKULD	Coming to the hall to feast on men's flesh.
URD	The great hall itself standing in darkness.
VEDANDI	No sound of laughter.
SKULD	No song of harp.
URD	Only the sound of the country weeping.
VEDANDI	Like the weeping of the wind through dead grass.
SKULD	So it shall go on.
URD	So it must go on.
VEDANDI	A doom from which none can escape.
SKULD	Men's doom to suffer the rage of the beast. 190
URD	The beast's doom to be the cause of their suffering.
VEDANDI	Man and beast bound in doom together.
SKULD	Until one shall come to set them free.
URD	From across the sea, following the whale-track.
VEDANDI	The man whose tale we're telling.
SKULD	Whose life we're weaving.
URD	Whose fate we're making.
VEDANDI	The outlaw, the outcast.
SKULD	The stranger, the hero.

Scene 2 • Beowulf arrives in the land of the Scyldings

The COASTGUARD enters onto the raised platform. He speaks to the audience.

COASTGUARD This cold will be the death of me. Day and night I keep watch up here on this headland. And if the days are bad, the nights are worse – frost in the air, the ground like iron, flesh that aches and a wind that bites. It's got a tooth sharp as any wolf's fang. Up there in the sky the stars glitter like pieces of ice. And though the moon gives light, she gives no comfort. I'm frozen through, chilled to the bone. And for what reason? None that I can see. Keep a lookout for strangers, enemies approaching. Those are my orders. In the old days there might have been good cause. But now? What stranger ever sets foot here in Denmark? Our country's shunned, a cursed land. And our only enemy lies within. An enemy that all fear. A beast that holds the land fast in its grip. Grendel.

The FATES whisper the name softly, eerily.

URD Grendel.

VEDANDI Grendel.

SKULD Grendel.

COASTGUARD What? What's that I heard?

URD Moor-stalker.

VEDANDI Shadow-creeper.

SKULD Night-walker.

COASTGUARD Voices? Who is it? Who's speaking?

URD Blood-drinker.

VEDANDI Bone-breaker.

ACT I SCENE 2

SKULD	Death-bringer.	
COASTGUARD	Who's out there?	
URD	Grendel.	
VEDANDI	Grendel.	
SKULD	Grendel.	30
COASTGUARD	Only the wind. But I thought it spoke the monster's name. Whispering down there through the frozen grass. I'd curse it, but it's already cursed. And we're cursed too. It blights our whole country, that curse, a dark shadow cast on each one of us that lives here. Up there, on the hilltop, the King's great hall. Heorot. I remember when it was first built. A magnificent place, nothing like it seen before. It stands in darkness now, empty, abandoned, a place of terror. And there's only one king there. Grendel.	
	The FATES whisper again, together.	40
FATES	Grendel.	
COASTGUARD	That wind's getting sharper. But it's blowing the night away. Look, there, on the skyline, a band of light brightening the wavetops. Growing broader, deeper. It's a good sight. No matter how low your spirits they lift with the sunrise. And each new day brings the promise of hope, even if it's only the barest scrap… Wait! What's that? What is it there? Coming up with the sun over the horizon – something shining, flashing… There's a sail! And a curved prow! It's a ship! A ship coming this way, out of the east! Heading right for this shore! Who's sailing it? What men are aboard? Where are they from? Are they enemies or friends? Only one way to find out, go down there and ask them. Then we'll know what kind of men these are. And what strangers might want in our doomed land.	50
	The COASTGUARD climbs down from the platform, as GEAT WARRIORS enter.	

10

ACT I SCENE 2

GEATS	We come from over the sea, the land of the Geats
	From there we've travelled, taking the whale-road
	Sunrise to sunrise, a day's good sailing **60**
	Like a bird the craft sped, skimming the wave-tops
	Curved prow cutting a path through the water
	Till at last land was sighted, the journey was ended
	We lowered the sail, steered the ship in
	Leapt out in the shallows, dragged it onto the shore
	Made it secure, fixed fast with a rope
	Now we stand on this foreign ground
	Firm-footed, hard-eyed
	Men with a purpose.
	The COASTGUARD has now descended and approaches them. **70**
COASTGUARD	And what is that purpose? Eh? That's what I have to know. What's brought you here to Dane-land? That's what you must tell me.
	BEOWULF enters and speaks to the COASTGUARD.
BEOWULF	I'll tell you. We have nothing to hide. A story brought us here.
COASTGUARD	A story?
BEOWULF	A story we heard in the hall of my uncle.
COASTGUARD	Who is your uncle?
BEOWULF	Hygelac, the Geat king. He's our lord. With his blessing I led **80** these men here.
COASTGUARD	Because of a story, you said…
BEOWULF	I'm sure you know it. It concerns your land. A horror that haunts it. A travelling singer told us the tale, one night as

 **Geats** *The Geats were the people of Geatland, which was in what is now southern Sweden. (See the map on page 81.)*

ACT I SCENE 2

	we sat in Hygelac's hall. He sang of a beast that comes from the dark, something inhuman, waging war on you all. We've come to see if this story's true. And if it is… perhaps we can do something about it.	
COASTGUARD	It's true, though I wish that it weren't. Grendel, this monster's called, and for twelve years we've lived under its reign of terror. Each night he sits up there in the king's hall, daring any man to come and try to throw him out.	90
BEOWULF	And do they dare?	
COASTGUARD	Once, they did. Men loyal to Hrothgar, his finest warriors. Others from further off who fancied themselves heroes. Men like yourself. None of them survived.	
BEOWULF	Your look seems to say the same doom awaits us.	
COASTGUARD	I won't lie to you, friend. If you've come to wage war on Grendel, I think it's a war you'll lose. Board your ship again, sail back home. That's my advice – though I don't suppose you'll take it.	100
BEOWULF	You're right. We won't.	
COASTGUARD	I thought not. In that case you're free to go on to Heorot. You can see it there on top of the hill. There's a road that leads directly to it. I'll go on ahead and tell Hrothgar of your coming. Farewell to you. I won't say good luck, because you'll find none here.	
	COASTGUARD turns and speaks to the audience.	
	There's something about this man that makes me uneasy. I can't say what it is. Something beyond words. He has the look of a man who's seen more than he should have. A light in his eyes, hard, cold. The kind you see in the eyes of a hero – or a madman. He's one or the other. Or maybe both.	110
	COASTGUARD goes. BEOWULF turns to the GEATS.	
BEOWULF	Secure the ship. Get your gear together. We're near our	

ACT I SCENE 2

journey's end, now. Let's make our way to Heorot.

The GEATS speak to the audience individually.

GEATS
We take the road north, heading inland
A well-worn track through hard country
The sun's up, but hidden   **120**
Its light pale and cold
And there's a grey drizzle in the air
It clings to our skin, damp, freezing
High cliffs rise up on either side
Grey crags split by roots and weather
And a grey sky above, heavy with cloud
It's a grim land we've come to, gripped hard by winter
But gripped by something else too
Something else has this country tight in its grasp
Fear   **130**
We can sense it everywhere
See it, almost
Something real, solid
Living, breathing
The whole land is like some frightened animal
An animal caught in a trap
Wounded, broken, unable to escape
The iron teeth of the trap closed fast on its neck
And it gnaws at its own body and grows weaker
And soon it will die unless the trap is sprung   **140**
That's what we're here for
That's our business, to spring that trap
So we walk on and come at last to Heorot
The gates stand open and we pass through them
Cross the courtyard
Past the cattle-pens, the sheep-folds
The blacksmith's forge, the outbuildings
And stop before the great hall itself
And we lean our spears against its wall
And stand waiting, stamping our feet against the cold   **150**
As our captain goes in to speak with the king.

ACT I SCENE 2

HROTHGAR, WEALTHEOW, ASHERE and UNFERTH enter and speak to BEOWULF.

BEOWULF	Lord Hrothgar, I believe you've been told already of my purpose in coming to your land.
HROTHGAR	It's been made known to me. But as to who you are – your name and family – that I do not yet know.
BEOWULF	Then I'll tell you. My uncle is Hygelac, King of the Geats.
UNFERTH	The Geat king, we hear, has many nephews. Some of them more reputable than others. Which of his brother's sons are you?
BEOWULF	No brother's son, but a sister's. Ursula, who married Ecgtheow, my father. My name is Beowulf, his only son.
HROTHGAR	Ecgtheow? I knew the man! Ashere, you remember Ecgtheow. Years ago he came here, when we were both young men.
ASHERE	I do, Lord Hrothgar. And, if I recall, he came in flight from his own land. Some dispute, I believe. A family quarrel.
HROTHGAR	It's true he came here under a shadow, but he proved himself a true man in my service. We often fought together side by side. I rewarded him well for the work he did here.
BEOWULF	I know that, Lord Hrothgar. My father spoke of you with the highest regard. "A true king," he said, "if any man is."
HROTHGAR	I was sorry when he left. I haven't seen him since. Is he still living?
BEOWULF	No. He's dead.
HROTHGAR	Fallen in battle?
BEOWULF	A family quarrel.
HROTHGAR	These blood-feuds are a curse on all our people. In building Heorot it was my purpose to rid us of such feuds forever. To establish a court where all disputes could be settled within

160

170

180

ACT I SCENE 2

	the law. That would have been an achievement. But it came to nothing. Grendel saw to that. Our feud with him has cost us dear in blood.
BEOWULF	I may be the man to bring that feud to an end.
UNFERTH	You? And why should you succeed where others have failed?
HROTHGAR	Unferth. Take care. While he stands under our roof this man's our guest. We would not wish to offer him offence.
UNFERTH	It's not my purpose to offend – but to judge his worth for the task he'd undertake. He says he's King Hygelac's nephew. And you knew his father. What do we know about him? Beowulf? It's not a name I've heard before.
BEOWULF	It's true, you know nothing about me. But let me prove my worth here tonight in Heorot. When morning comes, either I or the monster will lie dead. You can judge me then.
UNFERTH	Brave words. But how will you fight Grendel? No blade can cut him, no spear pierce his flesh. What weapon will you choose?
BEOWULF	None. I'll put my trust in my hands, pit my strength against his.
UNFERTH	(*To HROTHGAR.*) Feed this man and send him home, Lord Hrothgar. It's plain he's mad.
HROTHGAR	Before I decide I'll hear more. Ashere. You're my oldest friend and adviser. What do you say?

190

200

 **blood-feuds** Quarrels and feuds between rival clans and tribes were a common feature of Viking and Anglo-Saxon society. Each clan was like a large family, and had its own chief or king, to whom all members of the clan owed complete loyalty. Any insult or injury done to any member of the clan had to be avenged, often leading to years of bloodshed. This theme of the blood-feud – and the ultimate tragedy to which it leads – runs throughout the whole of *Beowulf*.

ACT I SCENE 2

ASHERE	This Beowulf is Hygelac's kinsman. If he should die here, in our land, Hygelac will be sworn to avenge his death. And if – if he should succeed in slaying Grendel, we find ourselves bound in obligation to the Geats. I'm sure you'll agree, Hrothgar, neither is desirable.
BEOWULF	I'm not here as Hygelac's kinsman, but as myself alone. There are no conditions to my offer of help. No obligations, whatever the outcome. All I have is my name. Beowulf. And if it means nothing to you now, perhaps it will in days to come.
UNFERTH	Yourself alone? What do you mean by that? Are you outcast from your own folk? Perhaps you come here as your father did, an outlaw?
HROTHGAR	Unferth! That's enough! You've said more than you should.
UNFERTH	And Beowulf, it seems to me, has not said enough…
BEOWULF	A man's not known by his words but by his deeds. What I say I'll do, I will do.
HROTHGAR	*(To WEALTHEOW.)* Wealtheow. You've heard our words. As my queen you have the right to add yours. What are your thoughts? Should we accept this man's offer of help?
WEALTHEOW	I see no argument in the matter. I think we must.
HROTHGAR	We must? Why?
WEALTHEOW	When you took me from my people and married me and made me your queen, what was the reason for it?
HROTHGAR	To settle the feud between your folk and mine. To bring peace to both our people.
WEALTHEOW	Why did you choose that course of action?
HROTHGAR	Any other course would have led to bloodshed – the devastation of your land and ours.
WEALTHEOW	You felt you had no choice? You felt it was the right thing to do?

ACT I SCENE 2

HROTHGAR	Yes.
WEALTHEOW	To accept Beowulf's offer is also the right thing to do – the only way of ending the feud between ourselves and Grendel. How long has it been since one of your own warriors stood watch in Heorot and challenged the monster? Who else, apart from the stranger, comes forward now?
HROTHGAR	You know there's no one.
WEALTHEOW	Then let Beowulf stand. And if some say, "Why should he succeed where others fail?" I say this in reply. There's something in this man I've not seen in any other warrior. He has a strength that lies deeper than blood and bone. If any man can, he'll prevail against the monster.
HROTHGAR	There's wisdom in your words. Beowulf, for your father's sake, and for the sake of Wealtheow's words, I give you leave. You and your companions shall take charge of Heorot tonight. And I pray to the gods it's victory and not death you find here.
BEOWULF	All men carry their deaths sleeping within them. They're fixed in us by the Fates before our birth. If mine chooses to wake here, let it be. Just send word to my uncle that I died a hero's death, and let my name be remembered for it.
HROTHGAR	You have my word. *(Turns to ASHERE and UNFERTH.)* Unferth, find quarters for Beowulf's followers. Ashere, see that food and drink are prepared for our guests. Tonight we'll feast again in Heorot.

All go, except for the GEATS, who remain onstage.

Scene 3 • The Fight in the Hall

GEATS turn and speak to the audience.

GEATS
And we gaze at it in wonder
When the feast's ready and we're finally let in
We have to admit it
This hall of the Scyldings really is magnificent
Even with all the battering it's taken over the years
Even though it's seen better days
We're awed by its size
The height
The space
The richness of its hangings
The craftsmanship of its carvings
And there's food laid out on the tables
And a good fire blazing
And wine in the cups
Everything's been done to make it welcoming
To make us feel like honoured guests
And then the Scyldings come in.

The SCYLDINGS enter.

SCYLDINGS
And we look at these people
These Geats from across the sea
Strangers from another country
Like us, but different
Stockier, something clumsy in their movements
A little rougher
A little readier
Awkward, somehow, and seeming out of place
And though they share our language
Their accent's different
A strange way they have of pronouncing words
Their voices harsher
More rasping and guttural

ACT I SCENE 3

	And these are the people we must welcome as guests	
	We must show these men all due respect	
	Because they'll kill the monster, so they say	
	As to that, we'll just have to wait and see	
	If they succeed, then they'll have earned our respect.	
GEATS	Seems like these Scyldings don't think of us too highly	
	They seem to doubt we're up to the job	
	They don't know us Geats	
	Our speech might be blunt	40
	But once we say we'll do a thing, we do it	
	Or die trying	
	As for killing this creature that haunts their hall	
	How come they haven't done it themselves?	
	Twelve years of terror and the monster's still here!	
	Where are all their brave warriors?	
	The best of them sleeping in Grendel's gut!	
	And we don't see any others volunteering for the job	
	It takes a stranger to get them out of trouble	
	A Geat, our captain	50
	Beowulf's his name	
	And it's a name they won't forget	
	Once he's shown them the makings of a true warrior.	
SCYLDINGS	A true warrior, is he, this captain of yours?	
	Valiant? Far-famed? Well-known for his deeds?	
	There's one deed we know about	
	A story we've heard	
	It seems that when he was a boy, Beowulf had a close friend	
	Breca, we think his name was	
	Beowulf and Breca, the two of them were inseparable	60
	And we heard that these two challenged each other to a race	
	A swimming race	
	In the open sea	
	Armed and in full armour	
	Crazy! But that's how boys are	
	So, as the story goes, they had this race	
	Both plunged into the sea	

ACT I SCENE 3

Both swam, from one headland to another
And the one who got there first was Breca
Beowulf, your captain and true hero 70
He came in second, a long way behind
That's the story as it's come to us
But, as you say, you can't believe everything you hear
So tell us, is it true?
And, if it is, where's Breca?
What became of him?
Nothing's been heard of him since
Why isn't he here?

GEATS Strange how stories have a way of changing with the telling
The further they travel, the more they're twisted out of shape 80
You've got part of it right, but the part that's least important
Yes, Beowulf and Breca had a swimming-match
Yes, Breca did come ashore first
But there's a lot more to tell than that
So listen, and we'll tell you what really happened
As soon as they hit the water a storm came up
Black clouds, thunder, howling wind, driving rain
The waves churned
The sea boiled
Beowulf and Breca lost sight of each other 90
And the storm woke something from the deep
A terrible monster, a Kraken
It caught hold of Beowulf and dragged him to the bottom
Wrapped him in its tentacles, tried to crush him
That would have been the end of a lesser man
But not Beowulf
He cut through the tentacles
Slashed them with his sword

 **Kraken** *In the folklore of Norway, the Kraken is an immense sea-monster that attacks ships. It is part-octopus, part-crab.*

ACT I SCENE 3

                Then killed the beast itself and swam back to the surface
                But that wasn't the end of it   **100**
                The fury of the fight woke other creatures
                Horrible sea-serpents
                Three, four, five of them
                Long, coiling necks
                Jaws gaping
                Terrible fangs
                Six of them, seven
                They writhed and lashed in the sea about him
                All the worst horrors of the deep
                Beowulf fought them   **110**
                Hacked through their necks
                Slaughtered every one of that hideous hoard
                And as the last one sank beneath the waves
                The ocean calmed, the clouds rolled away
                The storm was gone and he swam back to shore
                Of course Breca had got there before him
                But he hadn't been delayed fighting monsters
                From that time on the seas around our coast have been safe
                Travellers can pass through them without any danger
                You'll find no monsters in our land   **120**
                Beowulf killed them all
                That's the kind of man our captain is.

SCYLDINGS   What a fascinating tale, and expertly told
                Better than any skilled harper could sing it
                Exciting
                Thrilling
                Entertaining
                If it's true, your captain's certainly a man to be reckoned with
                Slaying all those sea-monsters
                How many was it again? Six? Seven?   **130**
                Eight? Nine?
                Or was it more?
                Perhaps we didn't quite catch what you said
                Or perhaps their number grows with each time of telling.

ACT I SCENE 3

GEATS	It's not the number that's important It's the deed that counts And when it comes to killing monsters, even just one We don't see any sign of that being achieved here We don't see any Scyldings who can boast of that It's been a long time since any has proved himself in war.	**140**
SCYLDINGS	If there's been no war to fight it's because we're so feared Our battle-savagery's well-known far and wide What enemy would dare to break our peace? There's a thing or two we Scyldings know about killing.	
GEATS	Your cousins, maybe, blood-feuds, cattle-raids, But for full battle on the field give me a Geat anytime.	
SCYLDINGS	Give me a Geat and I'll show him our battle-skill.	
GEATS	Will any of us do?	
SCYLDINGS	Choose your man and we'll choose ours.	
GEATS	What weapon?	**150**
SCYLDINGS	Sword or axe.	
GEATS	I'll trust in my sword.	
SCYLDINGS	Take it up, then! We'll soon prove which tribe is the better!	
	A GEAT and a SCYLDING warrior are about to fight. BEOWULF and HROTHGAR enter. HROTHGAR is accompanied by WEALTHEOW.	
HROTHGAR	Stop! Put your swords down!	
BEOWULF	Do as the lord commands!	

We'll soon prove which tribe is the better *Rivalry between clans and tribes was a common feature of Viking society, and the boasting display a common feature of feasts.*

ACT I SCENE 3

	Both warriors back off, putting their swords away.	160
HROTHGAR	*(To the SCYLDINGS.)* Is this the way we welcome our visitors? Is this how the Scyldings show hospitality to their guests?	
BEOWULF	*(To the GEATS.)* Have you forgotten why we came here? As friends, not enemies! You bring dishonour on yourselves, our people, and me!	
HROTHGAR	*(To the SCYLDINGS.)* Heorot has seen enough of blood-letting. We have a common enemy. To fight among ourselves is the act of fools!	
BEOWULF	*(To the GEATS.)* Death may come to us soon enough. If it does, let's die with honour, and not in shame.	170
HROTHGAR	*(To the SCYLDINGS.)* Go, now. The feast's over. Leave the hall. We'll leave for others to guard tonight.	
BEOWULF	*(To the GEATS.)* Find a place to sleep here. Heorot's in our keeping. And pray that you bear yourselves better than you have.	
	The GEATS and the SCYLDINGS go. HROTHGAR and BEOWULF speak together.	
HROTHGAR	You see how easily it happens? How quickly men can turn to murder. The shadow of Grendel hangs over us all.	
BEOWULF	Men don't need monsters to turn them into murderers. The shadow that lies in their hearts is of their own making.	180
HROTHGAR	Grendel has no heart! And its shadow is darker than that cast by any man. Lift it from us, Beowulf. Let Heorot stand in the light once more.	
BEOWULF	It's my intention to try.	
HROTHGAR	Give me your hand. *(HROTHGAR takes BEOWULF's hand, grips it.)* There's a strength in you. The strength of goodness. This will defeat the monster. It must. All my hope rests in you. *(Looses his hand.)* Goodnight, Beowulf.	

ACT I SCENE 3

He turns to WEALTHEOW. 190

Wealtheow?

WEALTHEOW I'll follow. I wish to speak with Beowulf.

HROTHGAR Very well.

HROTHGAR goes. WEALTHEOW turns to BEOWULF.

WEALTHEOW You believe you can kill Grendel.

BEOWULF Yes.

WEALTHEOW I believe so too. Was the story your men told about you true?

BEOWULF There was… some truth in it.

WEALTHEOW But not much?

BEOWULF No. Not much. Men will tell tales. 200

WEALTHEOW Yes. And they will kill. You spoke of the shadow that lies in men's hearts. I've seen that shadow and how it works in the world. I've seen my own country torn by war – its towns and farms and villages burning, the sky filled with flames and black smoke. I've heard the screaming of the wounded, the keening voices of the women. I've seen the fields of battle littered with the dead, my own brothers lying among them. I was the price of the peace that brought an end to that war, came here as queen to my brother's killer. And here I've heard men boast of their deeds in that war, heard poets sing 210 of its glorious battles, the valour of its heroes. Fine words, sweet music. They move the spirit to tears. And those tears blur the vision, and all that's remembered shines and shimmers, and all crookedness and horror is forgotten.

I've seen my country torn by war *Wealtheow's experience was a common one in a society beset by blood-feuds, war and violence.*

ACT I SCENE 3

She turns to BEOWULF.

Are you a man like them? Do you share this self-delusion with the rest?

BEOWULF does not answer. she approaches him.

Take my hand.

BEOWULF	*(Hesitates.)* My lady…	**220**
WEALTHEOW	Do you fear my touch?	
BEOWULF	No.	
WEALTHEOW	Then take my hand.	
BEOWULF	*(Hesitates still.)* You are Lord Hrothgar's queen…	
WEALTHEOW	And as his queen I command you! Take my hand.	

BEOWULF takes her hand. She grips it. As she speaks she grows more and more agitated. It is as if she is seeing in Beowulf what it is she describes, and it affects her deeply.

Yes. There is strength in you. But my husband was wrong. It's not the strength of goodness. There's another power, deeper. It's there in your eyes as well. You see the shadow and don't turn from it. You gaze at it unflinching. You know it for what it is. The darkness in the beast, the darkness in man. One and the same, no difference between them. You know this. And you know it because you have seen it… in your own heart…! **230**

She looses him suddenly, as if burned.

How did such knowledge come to you?

BEOWULF	I sought it, in order to be strong.	
WEALTHEOW	A man like you… I think he's to be feared almost as much as Grendel…	**240**
BEOWULF	Only such a man can kill Grendel. The darkness in me will destroy his darkness.	

25

ACT I SCENE 3

WEALTHEOW	And what of the darkness in you, Beowulf? Who shall destroy that?
	BEOWULF makes no reply.
	I'll go now to my husband. We'll keep watch through the night. I pray that day will not be long in coming.
	WEALTHEOW goes.
	BEOWULF turns and sits in the centre of the stage. He is upright, still. He closes his eyes. The FATES speak. **250**
URD	Night has fallen.
VEDANDI	A night without stars.
SKULD	A night without moon.
URD	Black, heavy, solid.
VEDANDI	A night like a great doorway.
SKULD	A doorway leading from darkness to darkness.
URD	And he sits before it.
VEDANDI	He sits not sleeping.
SKULD	He sits in waking, waiting. **260**
URD	Gazing into the doorway.
VEDANDI	Which is also like the eye's pupil.
SKULD	Through which he stares, eyes clear, unblinking.
URD	And he sees back to time's beginning.
VEDANDI	To the time before time's beginning.

 **And he sees back to time's beginning** Beowulf has a dream of how the world was created, according to Norse mythology.

ACT I SCENE 3

SKULD	The time of fire, the time of ice.
URD	Raging flames, boiling mist.
VEDANDI	And a body forming out of the mist.
SKULD	Ymir the giant, the first-created.
URD	Ymir the giant, who sleeps and sweats. **270**
VEDANDI	And out of his sweat other figures are formed.
SKULD	Ymir's children, who kill their father.
URD	Hack him to pieces with sword and axe.
VEDANDI	Then blood flows, gushing, and becomes the ocean.
SKULD	And his torn, tattered flesh becomes the earth.
URD	And his cracked, splintered bones become the mountains.
VEDANDI	And his gaping skull becomes the sky.
SKULD	And the whole of creation is a vast corpse.
URD	The sky, and everything beneath it.
VEDANDI	The world, and everything within it. **280**
SKULD	A dead body sprouting the fungus of life.
URD	And he sees the horror of it.
VEDANDI	And he sees the beauty of it.
SKULD	The beauty coiled within the horror.
URD	A small, shining jewel.
VEDANDI	A pool glittering in the sunlight under green leaves.
SKULD	And at the pool's edge, three women.
URD	And in the pool, a face.
VEDANDI	His own face, staring into the darkness.
SKULD	The eye's pupil, night's doorway. **290**

ACT I SCENE 3

URD And out of the darkness a creature comes walking.

VEDANDI And through that doorway a creature comes walking.

SKULD And he rises like a brother to greet it.

The massive figure of GRENDEL once more appears. BEOWULF stands and speaks.

BEOWULF This is what happened
This is how the monster met its death
All slept but myself
There was no sound
No splintering of wood, no cracking of timbers 300
Silently the doors swung open
And night entered
With its chill and its blackness and its smell of corruption
I saw him first as a huge shadow blocking the doorway
A shapeless mass of solid blackness
And as I looked the creature began to take form
And the form it was taking was that of a man
A man crudely hacked from some ancient block of life
And he stood there reeking of blood and murder
With all his crimes woven into the web of his being 310
And his name hung like a deadweight around his neck
And I rose and approached him and spoke that name
And gripped his hand as if in greeting.

BEOWULF turns to face GRENDEL. The GEATS come on, crying out urgently, to the accompaniment of drums and abrasive music.

GEATS We awake to this terrible shout!
A loud, howling roar!
And the hall being tossed about like a ship in a storm!
And it's all pitch-black and we can't see a thing!

Lights! Light the torches! 320
We can't! The fire's gone out!
Grab your weapons!
Where are they?

ACT I SCENE 3

> We can't find them!
> Get out of my way!
> What is it?
> What's happening?
> What's going on?

> Confusion everywhere, everybody moving
> Running about, bumping into each other   330
> Falling down, trying to get back up again
> And the hall keeps shaking like it's going to tumble
> And our ears are deafened by that terrible howling.

The GEATS become still. There's sudden silence. BEOWULF speaks again.

BEOWULF He tried to pull free but he couldn't
I had him in my grip and I had him fast
And he knew that my grip was death
Death because I knew him
Death because I saw into him   340
Saw the long years sleeping
The long years dreaming of being a man
Then the sudden waking to find himself a monster
A thing half-finished and thrown aside
And the pain and the rage at being what he was
Hating himself, hating men
But loving them too
Loving them as he killed them
Devouring them
Trying to swallow them into himself   350
As if by eating men he'd become one himself
But he couldn't
He could only ever be what he was.

So his hunger remained
And his pain remained
And his rage remained
Lodged like a hook deep in his gut
And he couldn't be free of it
Until I reached with my hand and ripped it out.

ACT I SCENE 3

Drumming and abrasive music. The GEATS call out again.

GEATS
What's happening now?
What is it?
What's the noise?
Something's screaming
A terrible scream
Like the earth itself screaming
And that sound
Something cracking
Splitting
Tearing
And there's blood everywhere
Suddenly there's blood
Blood gushing over us
Soaking us
Drenching us
We're drowning in blood
Gasping
Choking
And that scream
That terrible screaming
Won't somebody stop that scream!

Abruptly the drumbeat and music stop. There is silence.

BEOWULF
I dug deep, held firm
Something gave between us
A bond snapped
He tore himself from me
Carried the wound of himself back to the wastes
Left me with a bundle of bloody rags
The scraps of himself
His sacrifice
His offering.

GEATS
The scream fades into the distance
And there's no sound
Just a breath of cold wind

ACT I SCENE 3

A chill whisper shivering to stillness
And us in the darkness
Like men died and dug up again
Blinking
And wiping the blood from our eyes.

During the above, the three FATES have ripped the figure of GRENDEL into two parts. One part, the larger, is taken offstage. The other part, the smaller, consisting of an arm and part of the torso, is now carried ceremoniously to BEOWULF and placed in his outstretched arms. He holds the arm up and speaks to the audience. 400

BEOWULF I stood here in the dark! I faced the tormentor! Hand to hand we struggled together. I felt the strength of his grip. He felt the strength of mine. It proved the stronger. He struggled to be free but I stood my ground. I meant to kill Grendel and I did. His flesh burst, and his life with it. He fled howling to his den to die. I came with a purpose. Its end 410 is achieved. The monster is dead. I, Beowulf, did this.

The GEATS turn and go. BEOWULF turns and hangs the arm from one of the branches of the tree. He turns and stands, facing outwards.

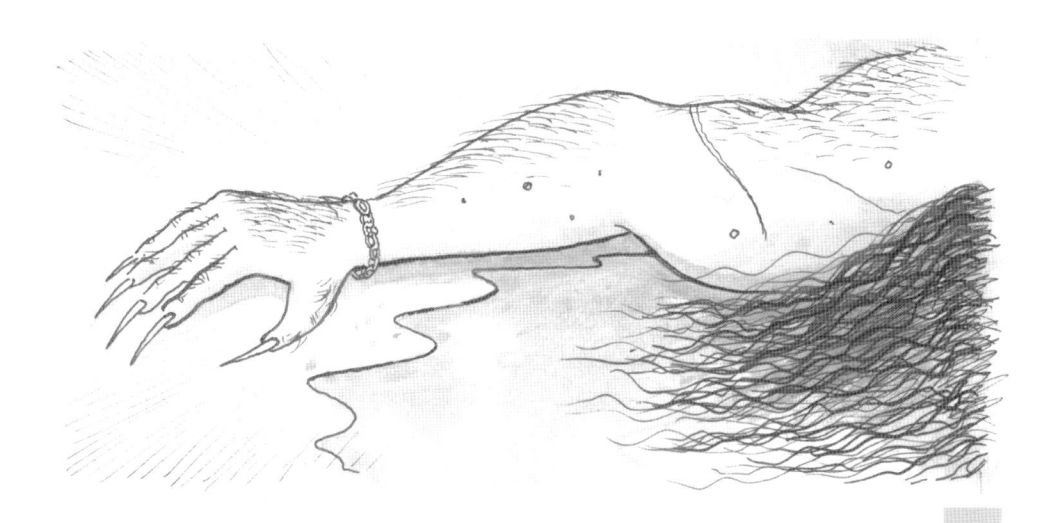

Scene 4 • Grendel's Mother

The SCYLDINGS enter. They sing.

SCYLDINGS   The monster's dead   1
　　　　　　　　Our land is free
　　　　　　　　This is the end
　　　　　　　　Of tyranny

　　　　　　　　A shadow came
　　　　　　　　A darkness fell
　　　　　　　　A creature crawled
　　　　　　　　From deeps of hell

　　　　　　　　It brought us blood
　　　　　　　　It brought us death   10
　　　　　　　　It froze our lives
　　　　　　　　With icy breath

　　　　　　　　We lived in terror
　　　　　　　　Dwelled in fear
　　　　　　　　Our days were filled
　　　　　　　　With bitter tears

　　　　　　　　The people wept
　　　　　　　　The country groaned
　　　　　　　　Grendel laughed
　　　　　　　　And cracked our bones   20

　　　　　　　　　But now he's dead
　　　　　　　　　And we are free
　　　　　　　　　And there's an end
　　　　　　　　　To tyranny

　　　　　　　　A hero stepped
　　　　　　　　Onto our shore
　　　　　　　　He entered through
　　　　　　　　The broken door

ACT I SCENE 4

In broken Heorot
He stood
Beneath the scratched
And splintered wood

And gripped the beast
And held him fast
Until the monster
Breathed its last

Grendel howled
And Grendel roared
His life-blood spilled
Upon the floor

Grendel groaned
And Grendel cursed
Sinews snapped
And bone-locks burst

A final cry
A final shout
And then his life's root
Was ripped out

   So Grendel died
   And we are free
   Of fear and death
   And tyranny

Wash the walls
And wash the floor
Cleanse the hall
Of blood and gore

Roast the meat
Prepare the feast
Beowulf
Has killed the beast

30

40

50

60

ACT I SCENE 4

> Repair the ruin
> Of the years
> When we lived
> In dread and fear
>
> Let the torches'
> Flickering light
> Burn the shadows
> From the night
>
> Let them flash
> Let them blaze   **70**
> Like the sun's
> Life-giving rays
>
> Now Heorot
> Shall shine once more
> Now Heorot
> Has been restored
>
> > For Grendel's dead
> > And we are free
> > And there's an end
> > Of tyranny.   **80**

As the song ends, other characters gradually fill the stage, speaking as they do so, with BEOWULF remaining at the centre.

ASHERE   So Heorot was cleansed of all corruption, and became once more a feasting-place for men.

UNFERTH   All gathered there beneath its high roof, to gaze in wonder at the monstrous arm, hung from its beam.

WEALTHEOW   And they ate and they drank, feasted freely and full, and their voices were raised in praise of Beowulf.

HROTHGAR   And Hrothgar the King gave gifts to the hero, many rich things finely made.   **90**

ASHERE   For always he was known as a generous king, free with treasures to those who served him.

ACT I SCENE 4

UNFERTH And Unferth gave him a sword. Earlier he had spoken against the hero. Now he took his words back and offered this gift. Its edge was keen, it had never failed any man in battle.

WEALTHEOW Around his neck with her own hands, Wealtheow placed a golden collar. A great treasure this was, delicately carved. And as her fingers fastened it about his flesh, so he was fastened forever to herself and her people. 100

HROTHGAR So Hrothgar clasped the hero in his arms. And he proclaimed him friend to the Scyldings till time shall cease. Then there was celebration in Heorot, voices raised in praise and song. And ancient tales once more were told.

The SCYLDINGS take up centre-stage to chant and enact the story of Sigemund and the dragon. It is a piece of entertainment performed for HROTHGAR and the rest, and should be exaggerated, even humorous, in style.

SCYLDINGS I sing of the hero, Sigemund the warrior,
Fearless in battle, brave in his war-deeds, 110
With his nephew Fitela he fought many monsters,
Grim ogres and trolls, they gave them reward,
Demons they set on the paths of their doom.
Always together they trod ways of danger,
And none with more hazard, none with more hardship
Than that which led them to enter the lair
Of the worm who dwelled in the dark of Earth's belly
Grim fire-dragon, greedy gold-gobbler.
Sigemund hacked a hole in the rock-face
Sought the serpent beneath the grey stone, 120
Coiled in the dark the creature lay sleeping,
Belly resting on a bed of gold.

I sing of the hero *Sigemund was another great hero of Norse myth. This story is also included in the* Beowulf *poem, and is meant to contrast with Beowulf's later fight with a dragon.*

ACT I SCENE 4

Sigemund woke him, wielding his sword-point,
Roused him to wrath, roaring, fearsome.
Flame burst forth from the monster's jaw,
A storm of fire, a searing heat-deluge.
Undaunted by this, Sigemund drove on,
Determined to win. It was warm work.
Then the beast lunged forward, broke through his defences,
Struck a sharp blow, sank fang into neck.   130
Sigemund reeled backwards, blood came pouring,
The wound was deep. The warrior fell.
Then Sigemund might have met his doom
Had not Fitela entered the fray.
He struck at the serpent with his sword's sharp edge,
Turned it aside, twisting, writhing.
Rearing upwards it roared aloud
A fatal blow locked in its jaws for Fitela
But Sigemund thrust hard at the open throat,
Delivered the death-blow deep in its veins.   140
Lifeless the creature crashed onto the rock,
Its days of guarding men's gold were done.
So Sigemund dealt with all earth's demons,
No horror could hold against a hand so strong.
Loved by his people, praised for his prowess,
He gained great fortune, even greater fame.

The SCYLDINGS move back from the centre-stage. The others speak to the audience, each – except ASHERE – leaving on his or her line.

ASHERE A good tale, it was. Good to hear it told, and good to hear men's voices joined in Heorot again.   150

UNFERTH And it was with good heart and full stomach that we left the hall, when it grew late and the fire burned low.

WEALTHEOW And we took our leave of Beowulf, and once more gave him thanks, for he had given Heorot back to us.

HROTHGAR And for the first time in many years our night was peaceful, and our sleep undisturbed by evil dreams.

ACT I SCENE 4

BEOWULF   And I too slept well. Weariness overcame me. I heard nothing in the dark. The Fates had planned it that way.

The SCYLDINGS lie down, sleeping, scattered around the stage. Only ASHERE remains standing. He speaks to the audience. As he does so, the FATES enter, wearing horrible masks. They approach ASHERE to stand around him.

ASHERE   I dreamed that night. I, Ashere, Hrothgar's oldest friend and counsellor. I slept in Heorot along with others. We lay ourselves down on beds of rushes, at ease and happy, bodies warm with wine. Sleep came easily. And as I slept I dreamed. I saw the wide moors under a full moon. All was lit and shining, each stone, each grass-blade, cut sharp and clear. And rising from the moor there came a cry, a single, wild cry, lifting up and out of the earth. A cry that froze the stars. They froze in terror as something came crawling across the wasteland, a shadow, shapeless, slithering towards Heorot. It touched the doors and they swung open. There was a smell of stagnant water. And like water the shadow poured into the hall, thick, black, clogging, choking. And I, Ashere, lay unable to move, as the shadow poured itself round me and over me, flowed into my throat, filling me with its darkness. And as I struggled for breath I woke, and the shadow was there and this was no dream. A hand clutched my throat. Breath rattled and croaked. A voice hissed in my ear.

The FATES speak softly, dreadfully.

URD   Vengeance!

VEDANDI   Vengeance!

SKULD   Vengeance!

ASHERE   Then out of the darkness a face appeared, and it was a face of horror, and I stared into the face and saw no more.

The FATES cry out together.

FATES   Vengeance!

ACT I SCENE 4

                As they do, they take hold of ASHERE and blindfold him. They lead him offstage. UNFERTH enters. At the same time, the sleeping SCYLDINGS wake and jump to their feet.   **190**

UNFERTH   You saw nothing?

SCYLDINGS   No, Lord Unferth...

UNFERTH   Heard nothing?

SCYLDINGS   Nothing.

UNFERTH   Not one of you?

SCYLDINGS   None of us. We slept well last night...

UNFERTH   Too well, it seems.

SCYLDINGS   Lord Ashere slept among us   **200**
Just there, on the floor
When we woke he was gone
We thought no more of it
Not until we went outside and found the blood
Fresh blood on the ground
And a trail of some kind –
The track of some beast or creature...
Going away from the gates and out across the moor.

UNFERTH   And do you know where this trail leads? Did anyone have the courage to follow it?   **210**

SCYLDINGS   A few of us did
We armed ourselves and followed it
Out into the wastelands
Nothing lives there
There's no sign of life
It's a bleak, forbidding place
And there's a lake there, wide and deep
Black water under grey rocks
That was where the trail led
And that was where we found Lord Ashere   **220**
Or what was left of him

ACT I SCENE 4

	His head jammed onto a dead branch The rest of him torn and mangled… We buried what we'd found and came straight back We've only just returned Now you know as much as we do.
UNFERTH	You saw no sign of what it was that did this terrible thing?
SCYLDINGS	Only the trail It stopped at the water's edge Whatever it was lives down there 230 It lives beneath that black water I wouldn't like to be the one who goes down there to find it.
UNFERTH	This is grim news. Lord Hrothgar must be told. But when he hears it… I fear it won't work well on him…
	HROTHGAR and WEALTHEOW enter.
HROTHGAR	Even so, Unferth, he must be told. *(UNFERTH turns and sees HROTHGAR.)* Tell me. Is Ashere dead?
UNFERTH	Yes. These men found his body.
HROTHGAR	Where?
UNFERTH	By a lake's edge. In the wastelands… 240
HROTHGAR	Grendel's lair!
UNFERTH	That's my fear too. The monster's still living…
HROTHGAR	But how can that be? Beowulf killed him…
UNFERTH	Grendel fled, wounded. We didn't see him die. Perhaps Beowulf only wounded him…
	BEOWULF enters.
BEOWULF	Grendel's dead. I killed him.
UNFERTH	So you've told us…
BEOWULF	I've told you what's true.

ACT I SCENE 4

UNFERTH	What you think is true.	250
BEOWULF	What I know to be true. I held him in my grip. I felt his life break. He did not survive our meeting.	
HROTHGAR	Then how do you account for what's happened here?	
BEOWULF	I don't, Lord Hrothgar. I can't. But my word to you holds good. I did not fail you.	
WEALTHEOW	Beowulf speaks the truth. Listen to him, Hrothgar. And listen to me. I think I can account for Ashere's death.	
HROTHGAR	How?	
WEALTHEOW	Grendel was not the only foul thing spawned in those dark waters. There was – there is – another. Older than he, ancient and wicked. Not male, but female. Grendel's mother.	260
	The SCYLDINGS speak.	
SCYLDINGS	We listen as she tells us what she knows What she's heard from the women of the country Peasant wives and daughters who tell these tales And whose voices too often go unheard These women speak of two who walk Wanderers across the moors and fells Grim night-stalkers Feeding on the blood of living things… Sheep snatched from pens… Babies snatched from cots… Late travellers who have lost their way… And whether they are trolls… Or goblins… Wights… Ogres…	270

> **Wights** In Norse mythology, a spirit that inhabited the graves of dead warriors and kings.

40

ACT I SCENE 4

	Or werewolves…
	No one knows…
WEALTHEOW	One they called Grendel a demon born of darkness. He they feared. But she, the other, they gave no name. And she is, they say, the more terrible of the two.
SCYLDINGS	In ancient times, the stories tell
	A man came to the wasted lands
	An outcast, outlaw
	Crimes heavy on his head
	There he met with her
	There she took him in her hateful grasp
	There they coupled
	Grendel the monstrous outcome of this grotesque union
	Of the man no more is known
	A hideous death was his fate
	But these two since that time have lived alone
	The fell and fen…
	The wolf-crag and the mere their home…
WEALTHEOW	And it's this nameless one, this mother, who bears the guilt for this new crime. She came seeking vengeance for her child's death. And she'll seek it again, until she's stopped.
HROTHGAR	Unferth. Give orders to our soldiers. Tell them to burn Heorot.
UNFERTH	Lord Hrothgar…?
HROTHGAR	Burn it to the ground. Scatter its ashes on the waves. Leave the earth to darkness and despair. There's nothing more for us here. It's plain the fates have marked us out for doom.
UNFERTH	Lord Hrothgar. Is this the way of the Scyldings? To give up while there are still men left to fight?
HROTHGAR	What men, Unferth? Who can we ask to fight this enemy? Send a man to certain death? I can't make such a request. If any man must fight it should be me. There's a bond between a king and his people. I won't be the one to break it. Bring

ACT I SCENE 4

	me weapons. I'll go.
BEOWULF	A king shouldn't risk his life when there's another to stand in his place. I came here to do a job and I'll finish it.
WEALTHEOW	No, Beowulf. We can't ask this of you…
BEOWULF	And it's unasked that I go, Lady Wealtheow. No one makes this request of Beowulf but Beowulf himself. What else are we here for in this world, but to find fame in risking all? Life without risk is no life at all. While we stand in the light, let's stand firm, and turn our eyes unblinking to the sun. When he's dead, all that remains of a man is his name. How it's remembered, good or bad, depends on his deeds.
HROTHGAR	Once more our safety lies in your hands, Beowulf. If you succeed, you'll be rewarded as before, gifts even greater than those already given.
BEOWULF	It's not wealth I want, Hrothgar. What gifts I have, and those to come, belong by right to Hygelac my king. But there's one gift I will make use of. Your sword, Unferth. I'll use it in this fight. Take mine for safe-keeping.
	He gives his sword to UNFERTH.
	If I don't return, cross the sea to my homeland, place it in my uncle's hands – and give good report of me.
UNFERTH	I'll do that, Beowulf. You have my word.
BEOWULF	There's no more to be said. I'll call my men. They'll go with me across the wastelands, keep watch as I seek out this demon, destroy her if I can. If it's my doom to die, you'll learn the news from them.

> **When he's dead, all that remains of a man is his name**
> There was no real hope of any sort of life or reward after death in Norse religious belief. In a society based on clan loyalty and war, a man's greatest hope was to be remembered well by his fellows.

ACT I SCENE 4

BEOWULF turns away, steps forward, and stands impassive, gazing outwards.

SCYLDINGS We watch them leave
Walking out through the gates 340
Taking the track that leads across the moors
The cold light of early morning folds about them
A pale shroud into which they're disappearing
A shiver runs through us, head to heart
We know the place they're going to
We've walked that track
Know where it leads, and ends…
That plunge downwards into dark waters…
That bottomless drop…
And it seems to us it's the kind of place 350
From which no man can ever return.

The SCYLDINGS go. HROTHGAR, WEALTHEOW and UNFERTH speak to the audience.

HROTHGAR And they disappear into the morning mist…

HROTHGAR goes.

WEALTHEOW Like ghosts fading, lost from the world…

WEALTHEOW goes.

UNFERTH And we don't think to see them come again.

UNFERTH goes.

BEOWULF now is alone onstage. He describes his descent into the lake. 360

BEOWULF We came to the lake's edge. The water boiled, thick and bloody. I gave my men orders to wait until nightfall. If I'd not returned by then, to go back to Heorot, take our ship home. Then I strapped on my armour, took the sword in my hand, stepped forward and plunged into the water. It was black and cold. I sank quickly, heavily. My lungs burned, chest ached, muscles knotted. I was held in a fist, being

ACT I SCENE 4

crushed. The blackness poured itself into me, filling me up. For a time I knew nothing. I ceased to be, became part of the blackness. Then, a scream of light, explosion of air, the weight of my body tumbling about me. I lay still. I breathed. My heart beat. I opened my eyes, raised myself to my feet, and saw that I was standing in a vast cavern. 370

The FATES enter, speaking.

URD Hollowed from bedrock, lit and glimmering.

VEDANDI Shimmering with blood-light, the world's stone womb.

SKULD The place of reckoning, the place of destiny.

BEOWULF calls out.

BEOWULF Who's there? 380

URD He calls, and his voice echoes.

VEDANDI His words flutter like bats in the shadows.

SKULD She hears them – and she answers.

GRENDEL'S MOTHER enters. She is a huge, amorphous, almost shapeless mass, something ancient and primitive, endlessly flowing and moving. Her voice, too, when she speaks, has an amorphous and liquid quality.

GRENDEL'S MOTHER Who asks? Who speaks? Who comes here?

BEOWULF turns to face her.

BEOWULF I do. Beowulf. 390

GRENDEL'S MOTHER A man, is it?

BEOWULF Yes – a man.

GRENDEL'S MOTHER What does this man want here? Why does he come? For what purpose, to my lair?

BEOWULF To destroy you – end your life.

GRENDEL'S MOTHER Destroy me? How can you destroy me?

ACT I SCENE 4

BEOWULF As I destroyed your son.

GRENDEL'S MOTHER Him destroyed? Grendel? Is he destroyed?

BEOWULF Yes. We fought in the hall and I killed him.

GRENDEL'S MOTHER Killed him? You have his body? 400

BEOWULF No – he fled, wounded…

GRENDEL'S MOTHER Where did he fly?

BEOWULF To this place…

GRENDEL'S MOTHER Do you see him? Is his body here?

BEOWULF No…

GRENDEL'S MOTHER Where is it, then, if he is destroyed?

BEOWULF Where is he if he is not?

GRENDEL'S MOTHER Gone. Gone far – and near. Always we are near. You know this. You would seek him? Look in your own heart. Perhaps he is there. 410

BEOWULF It's not him I seek, but you! Here, now, in this place! I ended your son's life, and I will end yours!

GRENDEL'S MOTHER Listen, man. Listen to me. Hear what I say. We cannot die. We have always been here. From beginning and before beginning. To end and after end. We are the darkness you crawled from, the darkness to which you will return.

BEOWULF No more words! Let action speak for me! If you live, then you can die. My sword's edge will prove that.

He swings his sword at GRENDEL'S MOTHER.

GRENDEL'S MOTHER We cannot be killed! 420

He swings the sword again.

When you think you kill us you make us stronger!

He swings the sword again.

ACT I SCENE 4

Always we return!

He swings the sword again.

To haunt your homes!

He swings the sword again.

To haunt your dreams!

He swings the sword again.

To eat your hearts! 430

He swings the sword again.

To dwell in you.

He swings the sword again.

Always and always we shall return!

He swings the sword again.

Because you call us!

He swings the sword again.

Because you need us!

He swings the sword again.

Because we make you what you are! 440

BEOWULF swings and strikes at GRENDEL'S MOTHER. She gives a loud, long wailing cry. BEOWULF falls to his knees, dropping the sword. Her body swirls about him, enveloping him. Then she disappears. Her cry draws away and fades slowly to silence.

The FATES step forward.

> **Because we make you what you are!** In other words, the warrior needs monsters in order to achieve great deeds and become a hero.

ACT I SCENE 4

URD	The cave's empty. She's gone.
VEDANDI	No sign, no trace.
SKULD	And the light flickering, slowly fading.
	BEOWULF speaks to himself.
BEOWULF	Where is she? Dead? Did I kill her? I struck with my sword… 450
	He looks round for his sword. URD picks it up.
URD	There is no sword.
VEDANDI	It's broken, blade melted.
SKULD	Boiled by her blood.
BEOWULF	Her blood? Her blood spilled…? I struck – her blood spilled… The blade melted – she's dead! I killed her! I, Beowulf! Once more I made good my word. I did what I set out to do. I slew the monster and returned. I found my men still waiting by the lake's edge. The day was ending, the sun 460 setting. And with the light of that setting sun shining on our faces, we made our way victorious back to Heorot.
	BEOWULF remains standing centre-stage. The FATES return to their positions by the tree.

ACT I SCENE 5

HROTHGAR Take my hand, Beowulf, to strengthen that bond.

WEALTHEOW And mine, to make it fast.

They each grasp one of BEOWULF's hands. All freeze, as BEOWULF speaks to the audience.

BEOWULF I took their hands – and their deaths gripped me. A black snake staring out through my eyes, gazing into the doom to come. Heorot stood in ruins. Smoke like a tattered flag hanging above it. Old grievances and jealousies walked the land like monsters. Sword-edge, axe-blade, the bloody wreckage of battle. Fields of bodies where the wolf and the crow grew fat. And Hrothgar dead, a knife in his throat. And his sons slain about him. And Wealtheow cradling her sons' bodies, crazed with grief, a madwoman weeping. And a shadow over the whole kingdom, rising up and out of it, shapeless, formless. And the kingdom of the Scyldings lost in darkness. And I heard this sound – soft laughter. 70

The FATES come forward. 80

URD And after the laughter – silence.

URD takes hold of UNFERTH and leads him off.

VEDANDI The dumb mouth, the blind eye.

VEDANDI takes hold of HROTHGAR and leads him off.

SKULD The heart stilled under the cold stone.

SKULD takes hold of WEALTHEOW and leads her off.

GEATS Now we're off with the next sun's rising
Shouldering our gear, making farewells 90

And I hear this sound – soft laughter In the world of the poem, and the play, there is only one eventual outcome to all life: death. This is the ultimate fate of all that lives. Part of Beowulf's strength is his ability to see this clearly, and to entertain no false illusions.

ACT I SCENE 5

                Taking the road that leads out of Heorot
                The home-road back to the coast
                And it's a fine morning, warm and clear
                A smoky mist rising up off the ground
                The warm breath of the earth, like the steam off cattle
                And someone cracks a joke and we're all laughing
                And still laughing as we come down to the sea
                And there's our ship waiting where we left her
                Dragon-faced sea-bird riding the shallows
                So we're down on the shingle unfastening the knots   **100**
                Pushing her out
                Leaping aboard
                Taking up the oars and striking out
                Away from the land of shadows and monsters
                That country of nightmares and bogey ghosts
                And already we can smell home in the salt-wind
                Hear the gulls unleash long loops of welcome…

BEOWULF   And the sun's in our eyes
                And our sail's full
                And the ocean rolls us towards our home.   **110**

                All go.

End of Act I

ACT II SCENE 1

Swords clashed
Axes flashed
Spearpoints struck home
Wounds opened their mouths
Blades bit into bone
Many brave men fought
Many brave men fell
There was no shortage of slain on the field of battle

Then Hygelac our king was brought down by a sword
It cut through his neck, and he fell in the mud 50
Heardred his son was felled by an axe
He toppled earthwards like a bull, bellowing
And Heardred's brothers, each one was cut down
Spear-point and arrow-shaft took their lives from them
There they all lay, like a great tree uprooted
Trunk hacked through, all its limbs lopped off

Our kingdom a tangle of tumbled firewood

We would have given up, then
Cut and run
Dropped our weapons and turned tail 60
But Beowulf stopped us
His war-cry halted us in our tracks
We turned back and saw him
There he was in the thick of it
Standing alone, sword raised
And the light from the setting sun flashed from his war-gear
And his whole body was bathed in that blood-red light
As if the earth about him had caught fire
And he was standing among the flames
Flames that roared and leapt and lit the sky 70
Flames of beauty and destruction
And the heat from those flames caught our blood
And we ran towards them, shouting, joyful
And plunged into the inferno of battle.

ACT II SCENE 1

> There was no stopping us
> We cut our way through the enemy
> Laid about us, right and left
> Our blood was up and our hearts sang
> We showed them no mercy
> Made swift revenge for our king's killing
> The work was bloody
> We took no prisoners.

The GEATS turn their backs on the audience.

BEOWULF By nightfall it was over. Moonlight shone on the field of the dead. We left them unburied to the wolves and foxes, carried Hygelac and his sons back to the hall. There, we built wooden pyres on the hilltop, placed the bodies on top, raised our spears in farewell. Then we gave them to the flames. They burned long and brought us no warmth. Afterwards, we buried their bones, raised a barrow over them. And in the wind that took their ashes I heard a cold laughter, and the land was left without a king.

BEOWULF goes. OLD BEOWULF steps forward.

OLD BEOWULF So they chose me. Came to me and offered the crown. They spoke of my exploits in Hrothgar's land against the monsters. Of my leading them to victory against the Frisians. And I was of Hygelac's blood, his sister's son. Only I could lead them, heal the country's wounds. It was born into me, they said. My destiny to rule them. So I did. For fifty years. We lived well. We prospered. We were a strong people. A golden age, some called it. And so it was. Until the Dragon woke.

OLD BEOWULF goes.

Scene 2 • The Dragon wakes

The SLAVE enters. He creeps on, looks around fearfully, as he speaks.

SLAVE	I didn't mean to wake it. I was on the run. A slave, running 1
from his master. I had no reason to run. My master's not a
bad man. But it just got into me. Like a voice, nagging at me,
day and night. Run, it said. Break loose. Be a free man.
Those words, burning in me, like a fever. The only way to
stop it was to run. So I ran, and I kept on running. I left
behind the places where people lived, made for the wastes,
where I wouldn't be found. Crags and boulders. Waves
crashing over cliffs. And there, on the clifftop, a hill. Smooth
and round. And a huge rock set in one side. There was a hole 10
in the rock, just big enough to squeeze through. I crept
inside, followed a low passageway sloping downwards. Then
I saw a dim light ahead, glimmering in the dark. I went
towards it, came to a stone doorway. The light came from
beyond it, so I stepped through. And I was in a vast cavern
and it was filled with gold.

*The GEATS turn and speak. They move gradually to the centre,
creating the form of the dragon. The SLAVE reacts to their words, as
if he can see the treasure before him.*

GEATS	Ancient treasure 20
From another age
A time before this
Lost and forgotten
And in that time
A man came here
The last survivor

Slave Slavery was common in Norse and early Anglo-Saxon society. Slaves were often prisoners taken in battle or raids on other tribes.

ACT II SCENE 2

              Of his kind
              He brought this gold
              The wealth of his people
              He buried it deep   30
              The curse of his race
              He left it here
              He never returned
              The man became bones
              His bones became dust
              The gold remained
              A gleaming hoard
              The centuries passed
              Its light did not fade
              Another age came   40
              It flashed in the darkness
              Its brightness singing
              A shining voice
              That called to the Dragon
              And the Dragon came.

              *The GEATS are now centre-stage, in the form of the sleeping dragon.
              As the SLAVE speaks, he gradually moves towards the dragon, as if
              hypnotically drawn towards it.*

SLAVE   It lay there before me. A huge creature, coiled beside the
              treasure. Its scales shone in the light of the gold. Or did the   50
              gold shine in the light of the scales? It didn't move. Its eyes
              were closed. It seemed to be sleeping. I crept closer. The heat
              that came off it! Like it was some kind of furnace. Water
              dripping from the roof rose up in clouds of steam. I reached
              my hand out towards it. I felt the power, the energy packed
              inside it. A little nearer and I could have touched it. My

> **And the Dragon came** *Traditionally, dragons seek out hidden
> gold and take possession of it, guarding it jealously, although it has
> no use for them. It's almost as if they're the spirit of gold itself,
> breeding greed and envy and cruelty in human hearts.*

ACT II SCENE 2

fingertips just that far off. I didn't touch it. I drew my hand back, crept out of the cavern, made my way back to the entrance. I was outside again, in sunlight and fresh air. I stood on the clifftop. I heard the sea below. And it was only then that I realised what I'd done. When I looked down I saw it. I swear I don't know how it got there. I don't remember taking it. But there it was, in my hand. A golden cup.

The GEATS speak. As they do, they break up the form of the dragon, run to different parts of the stage in panic and terror.

GEATS   And the Dragon woke

From its timeless sleep
From its ageless dreams
It woke
And came crashing out of the cave
Roaring
Howling
Out of the earth
Spreading its wings
Like a blazing star
Scorching the sky
Like a flaming comet
Searching the world for its stolen gold
It fell upon us
A bolt from heaven
A thunder-flash
A lightning-crack
And it burned our farms
It burned our houses
Town and villages
It burned them all

Like a storm at sea when the waves rise up
And they come crashing down on mast and deck
And the ship's ripped apart
Its timbers are splintered

ACT II SCENE 2

And men are dragged down to drown in the depths
Then the storm passes
The clouds clear away
The sun shines again
The sea is calm
But there on the surface you can still see the wreckage
And there on the skyline, an edge of darkness
And you know that the storm is building again

So the Dragon has stormed our land 100
So our lives lie wrecked among its smoking ruins
And we know that this terror will come again
Night after night, without cease or let-up
Night after night, till nothing is left

They turn angrily towards the SLAVE.

And it was you who did this!
You woke this horror!
You brought down this devastation
You!
A slave! 110
A runaway slave!
Not just a slave…
A thief…
A killer…
You stole that cup
You raised the Dragon
Now it wants vengeance
It wants payment for the theft
You're the guilty one
So you must pay 120
Take him!
Bind him!
Drag him to the beast's lair!
Throw him inside!
Give him to the Dragon!
An offering!
A sacrifice!

59

ACT II SCENE 2

The SLAVE falls to his knees in terror.

SLAVE No! Please! I didn't mean to do any harm!

GEATS Whether you meant it or not, harm's been done! 130
The Dragon's waking was your doing!
Perhaps your flesh will take the edge off its hunger!
Perhaps your blood will quench its fire!

They make a move towards the terrified SLAVE. WIGLAF enters.

WIGLAF Stop! Leave him! There'll be no killing! Not like this. And not by you. This slave's death will achieve nothing – except to stain your own hands with blood. Listen to me. These words I speak are Beowulf's. Your lord and king. He's the law in our land. Put your trust in him. Your trust and your faith. He'll decide what's to be done – and whatever he decides 140 will be for the best.

The GEATS move back. WIGLAF speaks to the SLAVE.

You. Stand up. On your feet! Lord Beowulf wishes to speak with you.

WIGLAF pulls the SLAVE up onto his feet as OLD BEOWULF enters.

OLD BEOWULF Wiglaf. Is this the man?

WIGLAF Yes. This is the one.

OLD BEOWULF approaches the SLAVE.

OLD BEOWULF Show me the cup you stole from the Dragon. 150

SLAVE Here it is, Lord Beowulf… *(He gives the cup to BEOWULF.)* …but I didn't mean to steal it…

OLD BEOWULF Just as you didn't mean to enter the Dragon's lair.

SLAVE I didn't know…

OLD BEOWULF And as you didn't mean to run away from your master.

SLAVE That's right. I didn't mean any of it. Something… just got

ACT II SCENE 2

	into me… I couldn't help myself… you must believe me, Lord Beowulf!
OLD BEOWULF	I do believe you. And I know why you did those things. I know why you woke the Dragon.
SLAVE	But, Lord Beowulf, I…
OLD BEOWULF	It called you. It wanted to wake, and it chose you to be the one who'd wake it.
SLAVE	The Dragon?
OLD BEOWULF	This. *(He holds up the cup.)* See, Wiglaf. How it catches the light. A thing of beauty. Beauty and grace and light. Don't you agree?
WIGLAF	Yes. It is… beautiful.
OLD BEOWULF	Yet it's a thing of darkness too. A darkness within it. Look at it again. *(He gives the cup to WIGLAF.)* What do you see?
	WIGLAF examines the cup. He speaks with surprise.
WIGLAF	A dragon…!
OLD BEOWULF	The stem its tail, coiling upwards. The bowl its jaws, spreading wide. Open. Hungry. Deadly. A dragon carved in gold. A dragon of light.
WIGLAF	You said it called…
OLD BEOWULF	It did. The light calls and the darkness answers. It was light that called Grendel out of his hole. Darkness and light, beauty and death. Where you find one, you find the other. Always. And we're caught between them and must dance to their tune. *(He speaks to the SLAVE.)* You're not at fault. I find and place no blame on you.
SLAVE	Lord Beowulf…
OLD BEOWULF	But there is something I require of you.
SLAVE	I'm a slave. You can command me anything.

160

170

180

61

ACT II SCENE 2

OLD BEOWULF One thing only. Show me the place where the creature lies. Lead me to the Dragon's lair. When that's done, you'll be free to go.

SLAVE Free?

OLD BEOWULF Free. A free man. In exchange for this, I give you your freedom. *(He turns to WIGLAF.)* Take him, Wiglaf. Find him food and drink, somewhere to sleep. We'll leave with the sunrise. 190

WIGLAF and the SLAVE go. BEOWULF turns to the GEATS.

Return to your homes, now. I know what you require of me, and I'll not shirk it. Tomorrow I'll seek out this worm, call it to account, settle the score. It won't come away from our meeting unharmed. Go. Rest easy. Your lives and your land are in my keeping. Place your trust in me, your lord and your king. 200

The GEATS go. OLD BEOWULF remains alone onstage.

Scene 3 • Beowulf's dream

OLD BEOWULF steps forward.

OLD BEOWULF It's night, now. Darkness on the land. Stillness. Silence. No stars, no moon. Nothing to be seen or heard. Only myself awake. And the Dragon. The two of us, waiting as the world turns. Towards what? Death. That's the end of everything. It would have been good to end my days in peace, come at last to a quiet sleeping. But my doom's still on me, a heavy burden, there to the finish. This man shall fight with monsters. Beowulf the hero, Beowulf the king. Not at this hour and time. I'm cold. My limbs ache, my joints are stiff. I'm without name or title. Just an old man, standing alone in the dark.

WIGLAF enters.

WIGLAF Lord Beowulf.

OLD BEOWULF turns to him.

OLD BEOWULF Wiglaf. Is the slave well looked after?

WIGLAF He ate well, and now he snores among the beasts in the barn.

OLD BEOWULF It's a cold night. And the bodies of beasts give off some heat. There's many a time in the past I've made my own bed among them – and been glad of it. You'll see that he's woken early?

WIGLAF There's a guard watching outside the door with orders to wake him with the sunrise.

OLD BEOWULF Good. I'll need my armour…

WIGLAF It's being made ready.

OLD BEOWULF And my weapons.

ACT II SCENE 3

WIGLAF	Sword, spear, shield. You'll have them.	
OLD BEOWULF	And a horse?	
WIGLAF	The chestnut mare with the white star on her forehead.	
OLD BEOWULF	Her mother's mother was one of those given to me by Hrothgar, as reward for killing Grendel. The very one I would have chosen. Your thoughts jump ahead of mine, Wiglaf. You'll be riding with me tomorrow.	30
WIGLAF	I had hopes that I would.	
OLD BEOWULF	I'll take only a small party. A few handpicked men. You'll take charge of them. Wait with them at the entrance while I go down to confront this worm. If by chance the fight goes against me, do what you can to kill the Dragon. The safety of our people will be in your hands, then.	
WIGLAF	I'll do all that you say, Lord Beowulf – but… must you face the creature alone?	40
OLD BEOWULF	Yes, Wiglaf. I must.	
WIGLAF	There's a story you're fond of telling. The story of Sigemund, and how he fought a dragon. He didn't fight alone. His companion, Fitela, fought with him. Together they killed it…	
	OLD BEOWULF quotes from the story.	
OLD BEOWULF	"Then Sigemund may have met his doom Had not Fitela entered the fray. He struck at the serpent with his sword's sharp edge, Turned it aside, twisting, writhing. Rearing upwards it roared aloud A fatal blow locked in its jaws for Fitela But Sigemund thrust hard at the open throat, Delivered the death-blow deep in its veins. Lifeless the creature crashed onto the rock, Its days of guarding men's gold were done."	50
	OLD BEOWULF turns to WIGLAF.	

ACT II SCENE 3

	You'd have me as Sigemund and yourself as Fitela.
WIGLAF	Yes.
OLD BEOWULF	It would be good to have a companion – not to go down into the dark alone – but I shall.
WIGLAF	Beowulf…
OLD BEOWULF	Your father placed you in my keeping, Wiglaf. He was the best of warriors. A good companion and friend. The last of those who travelled with me to Hrothgar's land. I promised him I'd look after you as my own son. I think you'll agree I've kept my word.
WIGLAF	You have. And it's a son's duty to repay his father's care, to stand beside him in time of need…
OLD BEOWULF	It's a son's duty to do as his father commands! Without question!
	WIGLAF stiffens.
WIGLAF	Yes, Lord Beowulf. Of course.
OLD BEOWULF	Wiglaf, I've brought our people fifty years of peace. A good thing, but it has its price. The best of our warriors are dead, or have gone to other lands. None that remain know the ways of war. Those that go with us tomorrow are untried, untested. When I go to face the Dragon, I must leave one behind in whom I can trust. One I know who'll stand his ground, whatever happens. One who, if I should fall, can take my place. Not only as war-leader, but as king. And before a king learns to command, he must first learn to obey.
WIGLAF	I understand.
OLD BEOWULF	Good. I'll sleep now. Here, on the hall floor. My cloak will do for a blanket. Just like old times. Stay here with me. Wake me an hour before sunrise. And get some sleep yourself.
	OLD BEOWULF lies down on the floor and wraps his cloak around him. WIGLAF stands, watching him, and speaks to the audience.

ACT II SCENE 3

WIGLAF	I watch him as he eases himself onto the floor. Slowly, painfully. This simple act costing him such effort. Then he wraps his cloak about him and lies still. Already he's sleeping. I think of the stories I've heard about him, those told in the hall – and those told to me by my father. The hero who fought barehanded with monsters, swept the enemy from our lands, brought a golden age to the country of the Geats. Now he lies with a sunken face, his breathing shallow. So shallow I can hardly hear it. As if he's already passed from the world. And after him, what then? What will follow? I stand in the hall. It's silent, empty. Like the emptiness of the world without its heroes.

90

100

WIGLAF turns, walks away from OLD BEOWULF, lies down, wraps his cloak about him, sleeps.

The FATES enter. As they speak, they make their way to the ash tree and sit by the pool.

URD	The old king sleeps.
VEDANDI	The old king dreams.
SKULD	And in his dream, time turns backwards.
URD	Young again, he walks in the world.
VEDANDI	In a time before monsters…
SKULD	Before fame and kingship…
URD	He takes the path of his life's beginning…
VEDANDI	That leads to the place of the pool and the ash tree…
SKULD	Where we sit, weaving his life's end.

110

> **The old king dreams** Beowulf dreams of himself as a young man, and takes us back to a time before the play starts. We discover now why he was an outlaw, and that all along he has known his fate. This may explain something of his fearlessness in the face of Grendel and Grendel's Mother.

ACT II SCENE 3

The younger BEOWULF has entered. The FATES speak to him.

URD	Come closer.
VEDANDI	Approach.
SKULD	Come near.

BEOWULF approaches them.

URD	You have sought us.	
VEDANDI	You have found us.	**120**
SKULD	What is it you want with us?	
URD	Speak.	
VEDANDI	Tell us.	
SKULD	Make it known.	

BEOWULF hesitates, then speaks.

BEOWULF	I wish to know my future.	
URD	That's easily told.	
VEDANDI	Easily known.	
SKULD	All men know their future.	
URD	For all, there is only one future.	**130**
VEDANDI	A future that is no future.	
SKULD	Death. The one future.	
BEOWULF	But before death comes… before that end… a man may be nothing – or he may be something. A man may have a name in the world.	
URD	You wish to be… something.	
VEDANDI	You wish to be… known.	
SKULD	You wish to have… a name.	

ACT II SCENE 3

BEOWULF	All those things, yes.	
URD	What you will be you are.	140
VEDANDI	Your future rooted within you.	
SKULD	Stitched into your skin.	
URD	Folded under your bones.	
VEDANDI	Sleeping in the cave of your skull.	
SKULD	What we know we can make known.	
URD	But first, make something known to us.	
VEDANDI	How you came here.	
SKULD	The road followed, the path taken.	
URD	Speak.	
VEDANDI	Tell us.	150
SKULD	We are listening.	

BEOWULF In the world I'm nothing. I have no name. I am… the outlaw's son. I killed a man, an act of vengeance. I fled my homeland, went north to a barren country. For a long time I lived there, little more than a beast. Then one night an old man appeared in my cave. I woke and he was sitting there. Hunchbacked, ancient. I believe he was a god in disguise. If I wanted a name, he said, I must first dedicate myself to Odin. My sacrifice must be complete, total, as was the sacrifice of the All-Father before me. I hung in a tree for nine days. I 160
took neither food nor drink. Unblinking I gazed into the sun.

> **As was the sacrifice of the All-Father before me** The All-Father is Odin, king of the Norse gods. He hung for nine days in Yggdrasill, the world-tree, pierced by his own spear. In return for this sacrifice, Odin learned certain magic songs which gave him the power to take on the form of other creatures, and also the gift of all-knowledge.

	On the dawning of the ninth day a great bird appeared, an eagle flying out of the sun. It took me from the tree. We rose into the sky. We flew beyond the world of men. It set me down in a place of mists. There was no sound. I saw nothing. I began to walk. At last the mists cleared and I found myself here, by this tree, by this pool. I saw you. I stand now before you. I know who you are. You are Urd, you are Vedandi, you are Skuld. You are the sisters who weave the threads of men's lives. You tell their fates. Now tell me mine.	170
URD	Beowulf – the outlaw's son.	
VEDANDI	Beowulf – the man-killer.	
SKULD	Beowulf – the nameless one.	
URD	Shall be Beowulf – the hero.	
VEDANDI	Beowulf – the slayer of monsters.	
SKULD	Beowulf – the king.	
URD	All this shall be.	
VEDANDI	Fame, greatness, glory.	
SKULD	And for all this there is a price.	180
BEOWULF	A price?	
URD	There's always a price.	
VEDANDI	For each thing given…	
SKULD	A payment to be made.	
BEOWULF	What price?	
URD	Your death.	
BEOWULF	All men die.	
VEDANDI	But not all know the manner of their dying.	
SKULD	You sought to know your future – so all shall be known.	

ACT II SCENE 3

URD	Look into the pool.	190
VEDANDI	Gaze into its waters.	
SKULD	Your own soul's deep, where your death lies waiting.	

BEOWULF sits, and gazes into the pool. The FATES speak to the audience.

URD	So the old king dreams of the young man…
VEDANDI	Who looks into the pool and sees the old king sleeping…
SKULD	And waking from his dream to the day of his death.

BEOWULF remains sitting by the pool with the FATES as OLD BEOWULF wakes, rises slowly, stretches, looks around.

OLD BEOWULF Wiglaf? 200

He sees WIGLAF still sleeping on the floor. Goes over to him, gives him a gentle kick.

Wiglaf.

WIGLAF wakes with a start, rising quickly.

WIGLAF Lord Beowulf… I meant to wake you…

OLD BEOWULF We've both slept late. Look outside. The sun's beginning to rise. The sky's clear. And there's a fresh breeze. It's going to be a fine day. *(He turns to WIGLAF.)* Come on. Let's put on our armour, take up our weapons. It's a good day for a fight.

All remain onstage.

? **Your own soul's deep** *'Deep' is used here in the sense of 'depth' or 'deepness'.*

Scene 4 • The fight with the Dragon

Part of the GEAT chorus enter. They carry the weapons and armour for OLD BEOWULF and WIGLAF: helmets, corslets, swords, shields and spears. They speak to the audience, while placing the armour on WIGLAF and OLD BEOWULF, and giving them their weapons.

GEATS Now we will tell how Beowulf fought the Dragon 1
Our king and hero
How he went out with armour and weapons
To face this worm
Sent by wyrd to wreak havoc
Our lord was determined it should not live long
How with sword and spear he set forth to do battle
Grim-faced and stern, his armour flashing
He rode through the land
For one last time to make war upon monsters. 10

OLD BEOWULF and WIGLAF are now armed. The GEATS stand back on one side of the stage. WIGLAF steps forward and speaks to the audience.

WIGLAF We rode north. It was a clear day. There was frost on the ground and the air was sharp. Soon we saw about us the Dragon's devastation. Burned farms and villages. The earth charred and blackened. Then we came to the sea's edge. The Dragon's lair lay above us. We had to climb over the rocks to reach it. It was hard going. At last we stood outside the entrance. As Beowulf had promised, he gave the slave his 20
freedom. He spoke a few words to us, gave us our instructions. Then he shouldered his weapons and went into the cave.

WIGLAF moves aside, leaving OLD BEOWULF standing alone. He speaks to the audience.

OLD BEOWULF A long passageway leads down. I have to stoop. All light shuts off. The darkness is complete. I go into the darkness,

ACT II SCENE 4

deeper. As if descending to the bottom of the world, the place where all things begin and end. My own beginning, my own ending. The passage grows narrower. The air's hot and stifling. I find it difficult to breathe. My armour weighs heavy on me. It seems I've come this way before. Each step I take, already taken. As if I'm standing far off somewhere, watching myself. Watching this old man struggling blindly through the dark. I see a light ahead. It grows brighter as I approach. The light of gold shining in a vast cavern. I stand there in the cavern, before that massive heap of treasure. Apart from that, the cavern's empty. No sign of the Dragon. Yet I know it's close. It's here, but I can't see it. Even now it watches me, wicked eyes, a wicked heart. It's waiting for me to make the first move. And now I know I have a choice. I can turn back, leave the cavern, let the Dragon have its gold, live my life out in peace. Or I can stay, and fight, and die, here, now. But the choice is no choice. It's already been made, ages before. There's nothing else to be done, nowhere else to go. I give a loud cry and wake the Dragon – my shout of defiance against the world.

The DRAGON CHORUS enter, crying out, chanting. They represent both the fury of the dragon and the flames of the dragon's breath. They surround OLD BEOWULF, engulfing him.

DRAGON And the dark explodes
Bursts into flame
Flame with jaws
Scales
Teeth
Waves of flame
Wash over him
Winds of flame
Whirl about him
He's caught in a cage
Of searing heat
Trapped by bars
Of solid fire

ACT II SCENE 4

    And his weapons fall from him
    They're useless here
    Hope falls from him
    There's no hope here
    Nothing but flame
    And rage and hate
    And rage is the flame   70
    That roars
    Hate is the flame
    That howls
    The world has become
    A blazing inferno
    He stands at the centre
    Its only fuel.

The DRAGON and its flames rage around OLD BEOWULF. He sinks to the ground. The GEATS cry out in fear.

GEATS   We hear the sounds of the battle   80
    We feel the sounds of the battle
    The ground quaking beneath us
    The whole clifftop shaking
    And a terrible roaring
    As if all the demons in the earth were waking
    Stamping their feet
    Making the rocks split
    Then out of the cave a jet of fire
    That singes our eyebrows and hair
    And another spout   90
    Of flame
    Bursts out
    From the head
    Of the monstrous worm
    And we scream and shout!
    "The king's dead!
    "The Dragon's won!
    "It's the end for us if we stay here!
    "We'll be burned alive!

ACT II SCENE 4

	"Consumed by fire!" Then the worm itself appears! And we run!	100
	The DRAGON leaps forward, flames bursting from its mouth. The GEATS run. WIGLAF remains where he is. He turns and speaks to the audience as the DRAGON weaves about behind him.	
WIGLAF	I stood my ground. Even though all seemed lost, I didn't abandon him. What else can a man do in this world but stand firm and remain true? Beowulf taught me that when all is lost there's nothing more to fear. And so, without fear, without hope, I faced the Dragon.	110
	WIGLAF turns and faces the DRAGON.	
	It loomed above me, monstrous. I made no move, let it come closer. Powerful it was, but I could see it was weakened. Long, deep gashes covered its body. Still I made no move, let it approach, waiting the moment. It reared up, towered over me, jaws gaping, ready to strike. And then I struck. I drew back my sword and thrust it upwards, deep into the creature's belly!	
	WIGLAF strikes with his sword.	
DRAGON	The monster rears The monster roars Blood gushes out Black blood, boiling, It writhes and thrashes Twists and thrashes Crashes forward Twisting its coils Heaves and rolls And tumbles, falls Smashing over the rocks Plunging into the sea To sink, silent Beneath the waves.	120 130

74

ACT II SCENE 4

The DRAGON is dead. The DRAGON CHORUS go. Only WIGLAF and the wounded BEOWULF remain onstage. WIGLAF approaches OLD BEOWULF.

WIGLAF I found him in the cavern. He was slumped on the treasure-heap. Still breathing, but I knew he was dying. His body was gashed and burned. And there was poison in his veins. There was little I could do for him. I walked across to where he lay, knelt beside him, lifted his wounded body in my arms. Then he opened his eyes and looked at me, and spoke.

WIGLAF is now kneeling, holding the wounded OLD BEOWULF in his arms. At the same time, the young BEOWULF comes forward, and speaks his dying words.

BEOWULF My life's ended. Doom has led me this far and now it's done with me. I've achieved some things in this world, and now the price must be paid. This is the death I've always carried within me. All those I knew in my younger days have passed this way. I'm the last of that kind. I fought with monsters, I was a hero, a king. I did something to keep the darkness at bay. But always it comes again. Be watchful of it, Wiglaf. I pass the kingdom now into your keeping. And my name and my deeds. Don't let them be forgotten. They're all that remains when a man becomes dust.

WIGLAF And so he died.

WIGLAF lowers OLD BEOWULF to the floor and stands. The chorus of GEATS enter. Some carry with them a bier. They speak to the audience, gathering about OLD BEOWULF's body.

GEATS We carry his body from the cave
Take it to the clifftop
Lay it down there, gently,
Where the salt-wind blows and the gulls weep
Then we cut branches from a nearby wood
Trim them, lay them in a pile
Build a funeral pyre and place him on top

ACT II SCENE 4

It's evening now
The sun's setting
A few stars glimmer in the darkening sky
Their light reflected in the still sea   170
That's when we light the pyre
The wood's dry and it catches quickly
Bright flames burst upward
The fire rages, fierce, consuming his body
And a woman sings a song of lament
She lifts her sorrow high into the air
Long, wordless notes leaping skywards
Her song speaks for us all

Later we bury his bones
Place with them his armour and weapons   180
A golden collar given him long ago
His horse, which we felled with a single blow
Raise a mound of earth over them
A great barrow sealed with a stone
It stands there still, up on the headland
Sailors name it as they pass in their ships

Look, they say, a great king's buried there
He did marvellous things
He fought with monsters
He was generous, kind   190
His people loved him
And though he passed away
And though his age has passed away
As long as this world remains
His name will live in it
And his deeds will endure.

The GEATS lift OLD BEOWULF's body onto the bier. He is carried off in a solemn procession. WIGLAF follows them. The younger BEOWULF watches them go. The FATES speak to him.

URD   Is it enough?   200

ACT II SCENE 4

BEOWULF	It's enough.
VEDANDI	You accept?
SKULD	You'll pay the price?
BEOWULF	I accept all. I'll pay everything.
URD	Go, then.
VEDANDI	Return to the world.
SKULD	Become what you will be.
	BEOWULF bows to them, then turns and goes.
URD	So he goes from his dream…
VEDANDI	Into his dream…
SKULD	From his dream…
URD	Into his life…
VEDANDI	From his life…
SKULD	Into his death.
URD	He lives in the world…
VEDANDI	He passes from his world…
SKULD	As the world too must pass…
URD	As the moon and the stars…
VEDANDI	As the sun and the sky…
SKULD	As all that is must pass…
URD	Into the jaws of the wolf…

210

220

> **As this world too must pass** This looks towards the end of all things, when the world, and even the gods themselves, will be destroyed in a great battle. The Norse people called this final battle 'Ragnarok'.

ACT II SCENE 4

VEDANDI	Into the belly of the snake…
SKULD	Into the silence and darkness…
URD	And from that darkness another world will rise…
VEDANDI	As other worlds have risen before it…
SKULD	And that too will pass…
URD	All things will pass…
VEDANDI	And we ourselves…
SKULD	Sitting here by the pool…
URD	We too will pass.
VEDANDI	Only the tree will remain.
SKULD	Yggdrasill, the world-tree.
URD	The sacred, the eternal.
VEDANDI	The tree cannot die.
SKULD	It only remains.
	The FATES go.

230

THE END

Looking back at the play

The poem

Beowulf was first composed as an epic poem probably around the eighth century AD in one of the Anglo-Saxon kingdoms of England – either Mercia or Northumbria. We don't know who the poet was, and the only version we have of the poem was one that was copied down two hundred years later, around the year 1000. There must have been other copies, of course, but this is the only one to have survived, and it's now in the British Museum. Running at over 3000 verses, it's the longest Old English poem we have, and it deals with events that are part myth and part history, and which take place in Denmark and Sweden, around the fifth century AD. So it seems likely that long before it was written down, the story existed in oral form, spoken or sung by poets at great feasts in the northern lands, and travelling with them across the sea to Britain.

The poem was written in the language of the Anglo-Saxons, what we now call Old English, the ancestor of our present language. Old English is very difficult for most people to read these days, so the published versions of the poem tend to be translated into modern English. Here are extracts from three different translations of the part which described the monster Grendel coming to Hrothgar's hall.

> With the coming of the night came Grendel also,
> sought the great house and how the Ring-Danes
> held their hall when the horn had gone round.
> He found in Heorot the force of nobles
> slept after supper, sorrow forgotten,
> the condition of men. Maddening with rage,
> he struck quickly, creature of evil:
> grim and greedy, he grasped on their pallets
> thirty warriors, and away he was out of there,
> thrilled with his catch: he carried off homeward
> his glut of slaughter, sought his own halls.
> *translated by Michael Alexander, Penguin Classics, 1973*

LOOKING BACK AT THE PLAY

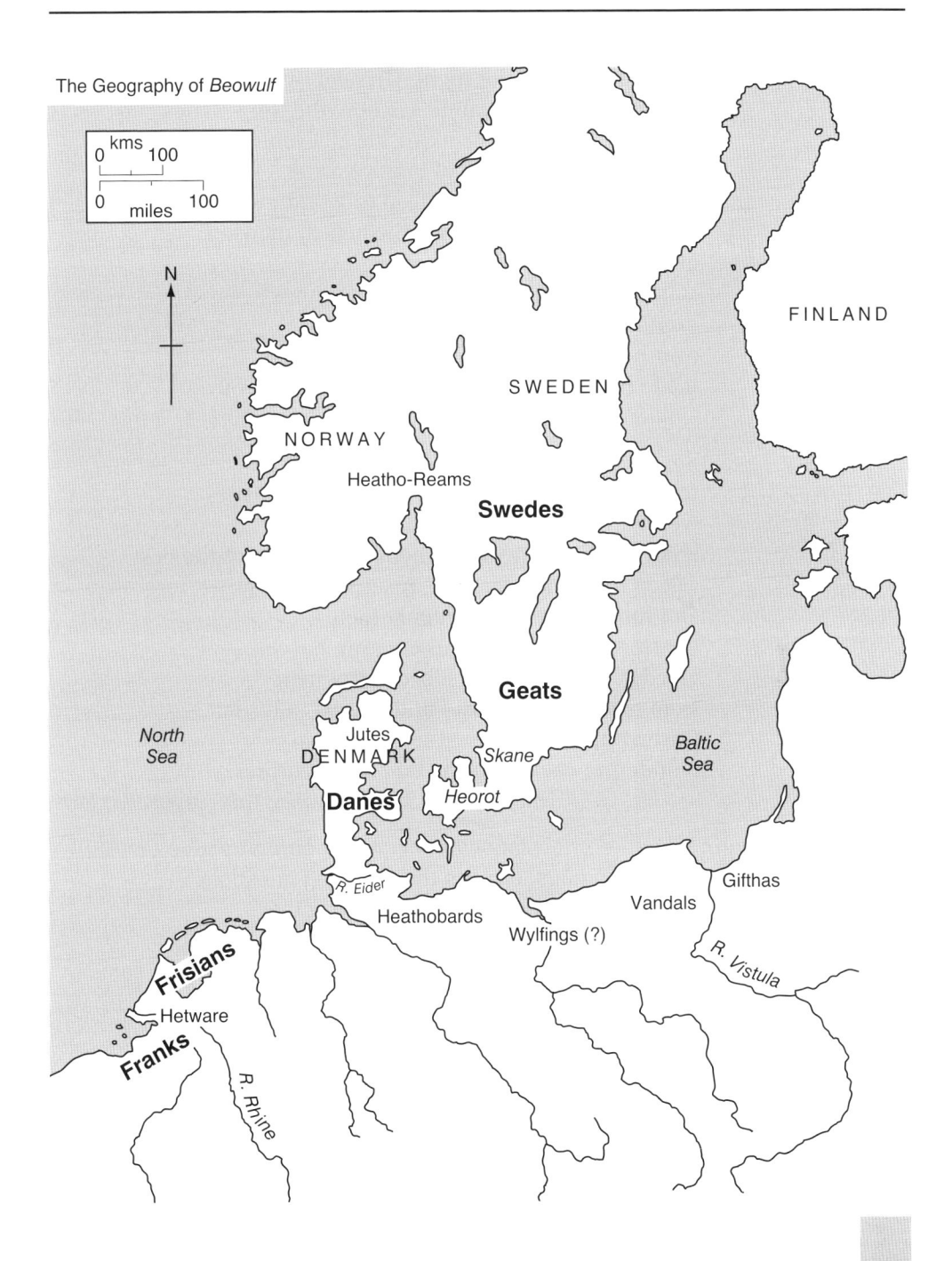

The Geography of *Beowulf*

- FINLAND
- SWEDEN
- NORWAY
- Heatho-Reams
- **Swedes**
- **Geats**
- North Sea
- Jutes
- DENMARK
- Skane
- Baltic Sea
- **Danes**
- Heorot
- R. Eider
- Gifthas
- Heathobards
- Vandals
- Wylfings (?)
- R. Vistula
- **Frisians**
- Hetware
- **Franks**
- R. Rhine

81

LOOKING BACK AT THE PLAY

> Then, under cover of night, Grendel came
> to Hrothgar's lofty hall to see how the Ring-Danes
> were disposed after drinking ale all evening;
> he found there a band of brave warrior,
> well-feasted, fast asleep, dead to worldly sorrow,
> man's sad destiny. At once the hellish monster,
> grim and greedy, brutally cruel,
> started forward and seized thirty thanes
> even as they slept; and then, gloating
> over his plunder, he hurried from the hall,
> made for his own lair with all those slain warriors.
> *translated by Kevin Crossley-Holland, Oxford World's Classics, 1982*

> So, after nightfall, Grendel set out
> for the lofty house, to see how the Ring-Danes
> were settling into it after their drink,
> and there he came upon them, a company of the best
> asleep from their feasting, insensible to pain
> and human sorrow. Suddenly then
> the God-cursed brute was creating havoc:
> greedy and grim, he grabbed thirty men
> from their resting places and rushed to his lair,
> flushed up and inflamed from the raid,
> blundering back with the butchered corpses.
> *translated by Seamus Heaney, Faber and Faber, 1999*

Read through these three translations a few times, so that you're familiar with them, and then, in groups, discuss the following questions:

1. How are the three translations similar to each other?
2. How are they different?
3. Are there any important words or phrases that are exactly the same in all three?
4. Which one of the three do you think is:
   - the easiest to read and understand?
   - the most vivid and exciting?
   - the best when read out loud?
5. Which one of the three do you like best, and why?

LOOKING BACK AT THE PLAY

Try writing your own description of Grendel coming to Heorot, either as poetry or prose, using a few of the common words and phrases in the three translations, but making the work completely your own.

There are several versions of the story written for children and young people. You might want to seek one or two of them out, and read them:
> *Beowulf: Dragon Slayer* by Rosemary Sutcliffe, Red Fox Books
> *Beowulf* by Kevin Crossley-Holland, Oxford University Press (this is a version for children)
> *Beowulf* by Robert Nye, Orion Children's Books
> *Beowulf the Warrior* by Ian Serraillier, Bethlehem Books

Heroes

Beowulf is a hero and a warrior. His life consists of fighting and killing, sometimes monsters, sometimes other warriors. There are many heroes like Beowulf in myths and old stories – Theseus and Odysseus, for example, from Greek mythology, and Gawain from the stories of King Arthur.

In groups, make a list of other heroes from myths and old stories. What qualities do they all have in common? You could write down your ideas as follows:
> A hero:
> - fights monsters
> - is brave
> - is strong

and so on.

Look through the play, and find moments when Beowulf displays one or more of these qualities. In other words, when he behaves like a typical hero. Make a note of these.

Are there times in the play when Beowulf doesn't behave like a typical hero? Are there qualities he has, and are there things about him, that make him different from the usual kind of hero? Again, look through the play, and make a note of these.

In groups, discuss what you think is the bravest thing that Beowulf does in

LOOKING BACK AT THE PLAY

the play, and say why you think this is.

At the end of the play, we are told that a woman sings a song of lament for Beowulf:

> And a woman sings a song of lament
> She lifts her sorrow high into the air
> Long, wordless notes leaping skywards
> Her song speaks for us all

Although her song is described as 'wordless', you could try writing the words for a song of lament for Beowulf, putting into it what his finest qualities and deeds were, and why the people will miss him.

Think of some modern-day fictional heroes. You can choose them from books, films, or television. Are these heroes the same as the old ones? Do they have the same qualities, or different ones?

Make notes about these heroes, and their qualities and deeds. Note the qualities that are similar to those of the mythical heroes, and those that are different.

You could try using the notes you've made to write a piece of poetry or prose called 'The Hero'.

Monsters

The story of Beowulf centres around his conflict with three monsters – Grendel, Grendel's Mother and the Dragon. Again, monsters appear in many myths and folk-tales, such as the Minotaur and the Cyclops from Greek mythology, and numberless dragons in folk-tales from all over the world. There are many different kinds of monsters – some of them animal, some part-animal and part-human, and some that look human but have animal natures. But are there certain qualities they have in common? What is a monster?

In groups, discuss those qualities that you think are shared in common by all monsters. Make a note of them, as you did with heroes:

LOOKING BACK AT THE PLAY

A monster:
- kills people
- is horrible to look at
- lives in wild places

Of the three monsters in the play, which do you think is the most horrible, or frightening? Write a short piece about this monster, saying why you chose it.

In the play, we're not really told what Grendel or his Mother look like. In fact, we don't really know what kind of creatures they are. We are told a little more in the poem. Here's an extract from the translation of the poem by Kevin Crossley-Holland:

> I have heard my people say
> men of this country, counsellors in the hall,
> that they have seen two such beings,
> equally monstrous, rangers in the fell-country,
> rulers of the moors; and these men assert
> that so far as they can see one bears
> a likeness to a woman; grotesque though he was,
> the other who trod the paths of exile looked like a man,
> though greater in height and build than a goliath;
> he was christened Grendel by my people
> many years ago; men do not know if he
> had a father, a fiend once begotten
> by mysterious spirits.

Imagine you're an eyewitness, one of those people who've seen Grendel and his Mother crossing the moorlands at night. Describe what you saw to some of your friends and family, and say how it made you feel.

You could then write this down as a poem or a piece of prose. Remember to try and make us see and feel what you saw and heard.

For me, the most fearsome and thrilling creature in the story is the dragon. It's certainly the most un-human of the monsters. In legend, dragons are solitary creatures that love gold, and they're to be found living in caves or within mountains, often sleeping on huge beds of treasure. Here's how the

LOOKING BACK AT THE PLAY

dragon is described in the poem, as translated by Michael Alexander:

> The Ravager of the night,
> the burner who has sought out barrows of old,
> then found this hoard of undefended joy.
> The smooth evil dragon swims through the gloom
> enfolded in flame; the folk of that country
> hold him in dread. He is doomed to seek out
> hoards in the ground, and guard for an age there
> the heathen gold.

Read the sections in the play that deal with the dragon, in scenes 2 and 4 of Act II.

As a group, speak aloud the Geats' lines from scene 2 which begin:

> And the Dragon woke
> From its timeless sleep
> From its ageless dreams

Or try the dragon's lines from Scene 4. Try different ways of dividing up and speaking the lines, to make the words as exciting as possible. You might also want to try adding some movement, or still images, to the speeches.

Make a collection of words and phrases you think best describe the dragon. You can take some from the play itself. Then write your own poem about the dragon, perhaps speaking as the slave who first sees it, or even speaking as the dragon itself.

Gods and Fate

The play opens with three goddesses, Urd, Skuld, and Vedandi, who control the fate and destiny of human beings. The people of the Sweden, Denmark and Norway – the Norse people, or Vikings – believed in many gods and goddesses, as well as other supernatural beings such as giants, trolls, dwarves and elves. In particular, they worshipped a family of gods and goddesses, called the Aesir. The Aesir made the earth, the sea and the sky from the body of a giant called Ymir. They lived in a vast, beautiful palace in the sky called Asgard. Midgard – or Middle-Earth – was the home of people, giants and dwarves. It was joined to heaven by a Rainbow Bridge called

LOOKING BACK AT THE PLAY

Bifrost. Beneath the earth was a place called Niflhel, a place of darkness where souls went after death, ruled over by a goddess named Hel.

Odin, also known as the All-Father, was king of the gods. His wife and queen was named Frigg. They had several children, among them the gods Thor, who rode a chariot across the sky and made the sound of thunder, and Baldr or Baldur, who was the most handsome and most loved of the gods. Frey and Freya were brother and sister, and between them they saw to the fertility of the earth. Loki was a god of trickery and mischief-making.

Although these gods were believed in for many hundreds of years, the tales about them weren't properly written down until the twelfth and thirteenth centuries, in Iceland, where the people of the north had settled some time before. These works were known as Edda, and took the form of verses and poems about the gods and goddesses. Also during that time, an Icelandic scholar named Snorri Sturlson collected these tales together in a work he called the Prose Edda. Much of our knowledge of the stores of the Aesir come from Snorri Sturlson's work.

There are many stories about the gods and goddesses of the Vikings. Using books, CD-ROMS and the internet, see what you can find out about them. Perhaps you could write down or tell one of your favourite of these stories.

The people of the north believed strongly in the power of fate. Their word for it was wyrd (from which we get our word 'weird'). A person's wyrd, or destiny, was fixed at birth, they believed, and there was nothing anyone could do to escape it. And it was not only people whose fate was fixed. All that existed had its own destiny, and that destiny always ended in one thing – destruction or death. Even the gods themselves were destined to die, and Asgard to be destroyed in a terrible battle at the end of time:

> The sun turns black, earth sinks into the sea,
> the bright stars vanish from the sky;
> steam rises up in the conflagration,
> a high flame plays against heaven itself.
> *from 'The Seeress's Prophecy', translated by Carolyne Larrington, in The Poetic Edda, Oxford World's Classics, 1996*

LOOKING BACK AT THE PLAY

Although, apart from the three Fates, the gods and goddesses do not appear in the play, they are referred to, and there is a strong sense of fate hanging over the heads of all the main characters. Towards the end of Act I, as Beowulf is taking his leave of Hrothgar and Wealtheow, he has a vision of the destiny that awaits them:

> Heorot stood in ruins. Smoke like a tattered flag hanging above it. Old grievances and jealousies walked the land like monsters. Sword-edge, axe-blade, the bloody wreckage of battle. Fields of bodies where the wolf and the crow grew fat. And Hrothgar dead, a knife in his throat. And his sons slain about him. And Wealtheow cradling her sons' bodies, crazed with grief, a madwoman weeping. And a shadow over the whole kingdom, rising up and out of it, shapeless, formless. And the kingdom of the Scyldings lost in darkness. And I heard this sound – soft laughter.

Look through the play and see what other references you can find to fate, destiny and doom. Make a note of all the words and phrases used that are to do with fate.

We discover, near the end of the play, that, early on, Beowulf has found out what his own fate is to be. What do you think is his attitude towards this fate? And what is the attitude of the three goddesses towards Beowulf? Why do you think they have decided to tell him his story? Discuss these questions in a group, then share your ideas about them with other groups.

The Vikings believed that our whole lives are ruled by fate. In other words, everything that happens to us has been fixed from the moment we're born. Do you believe this is an accurate view of human life? Or do you believe we're completely – or partially – free to control our own lives? Perhaps you can have a group or class discussion about this.

The three Fates are immortal spirits. They control the destiny of the other characters in the play. They should, therefore, somehow appear different from the other characters in the play. If you were staging a production of *Beowulf* how would you make up and dress the Fates? You can either describe this, or make a drawing of how you think the Fates should look.

LOOKING BACK AT THE PLAY

Words

The Anglo-Saxons were great lovers of literature and language. They told many stories and wrote many poems. Only a few of all those written have survived, but some of them are as vivid and exciting as *Beowulf*, even though nowhere near as long. They also give us a clear picture of what life was like in Anglo-Saxon society. We know, for instance, that they, like the Vikings, were great sea-travellers. Here's a short extract from an Anglo-Saxon poem called 'The Seafarer'.

> Wild were the waves when I often took my turn,
> the arduous night-watch, standing at the prow
> where the boat tossed near the rocks. My feet
> were afflicted by cold, fettered in frost,
> frozen chains; there I sighed out the sorrows
> seething round my heart; a hunger within tore
> at the mind of the sea-weary man. He who lives
> most prosperously on land does not understand
> how I, careworn and cut off from kinsmen,
> have as an exile endured a winter
> on the icy sea...

You might notice that many of the words and phrases in this extract use alliteration – that is, they share the same letter or sound:

> 'Wild were the waves when...'

> 'My feet were afflicted by cold, fettered in frost,'

> 'how I, careworn and cut off from kinsmen,'

See how many other examples of alliteration you can find in the extract.

Try creating some phrases of your own that use alliteration. It's probably best if you create these phrases around a particular subject to do with the natural environment – the sea, trees, mountains, the wind, and so on.

The poem *Beowulf* uses a lot of alliteration. It's also written according to very strict rules. The most important of these are: that each line has a short break, or pause, halfway through; that in each half-line, some of the syllables are stressed (or spoken heavily) to give rhythm; and that one of

89

LOOKING BACK AT THE PLAY

the stressed syllables in the first half of the line must alliterate with the first stressed syllable in the second line. It sounds complicated, but it works something like this. Here's a line from Michael Alexander's translation:

>With the coming of night / came Grendel also,

and another:

>So Grendel became ruler; / against right he fought.

Quite a lot of alliteration is used in the play, but this verse form is only used once, in the story of Sigemund and the Dragon in Act I Scene 4 – and not strictly even there. Pick out the rhythm of the line, find the breaks halfway through, and the use of alliteration, and mark the section as the lines have been marked above. Then try reading it aloud, emphasising all these.

If you remember that, before it was written, *Beowulf* was memorised and spoken orally, can you think why this particular verse form was used? Do you think it helps with memorising lines? If so, how?

Look again at the alliterative phrases you created. See if you can use them to write a short piece of verse, using this particular verse-form.

We call the language the Anglo-Saxons used 'Old English', and it is the ancestor of our modern English. Many of our words, especially those used for ordinary, everyday things, or natural objects, are Old English. Here are just a few:

>this, that, which, what, who, the, food, eat, water, stream, man, woman, walk, game, go, give.

If you look up a word in a dictionary (a big one, at least), next to its definition you'll find some letters in brackets, such as (F) or (L) or (OE). These tell you where the word derives from. So, F = French, L = Latin, and OE = Old English. Look through a dictionary and see just how many Old English words you can find. Make a list of them. See if it's possible to write a sentence made up entirely of Old English words.

LOOKING BACK AT THE PLAY

The play

The play uses a mixture of prose and verse. In the main, the verse sections are spoken by the Choruses of the Geats and the Scyldings. It's possible to speak these chorus sections in a number of ways. Here are some suggestions:
a) Each line is spoken individually
b) Groups of lines are spoken by an individual
c) Lines are spoken by two or more
d) Lines are spoken by the whole chorus

You can, of course, use a mixture of all of these, depending on the effect you want to create.

In small groups, take one of the Chorus sections and try dividing up and speaking the lines in a number of different ways, until you find the way that you think suits best.

When you're acting a character, you need to know something of the character you're playing – how old you think they are, what their personality is, how they speak, and so on. Write a brief character sketch of each of the following characters:

Hrothgar
Unferth
Beowulf
Wealtheow
Wiglaf
The Slave

Now choose the one you'd like to play, and write a more detailed account of his or her character, saying why you'd like to play that character.

How would you create the monsters on stage? They need to be believable, and truly frightening. Choose one of the monsters, and describe how you'd create it; or make a sketch of the monster, with notes.

Design a poster for a production of *Beowulf*.

Write a few lines for a programme, briefly saying what the play is about. It needs to be short and 'punchy', and make the audience feel they really want to see the play.

LOOKING BACK AT THE PLAY

Finally, how would you design a set for the play? The only item on stage mentioned in the script is the tree, Yggdrasill. What else would you have on stage as a permanent set? Remember that the play moves swiftly from one location to the next, and there won't be time for constant and cumbersome set-changes.

The Anglo-Saxons

The Anglo-Saxons first began arriving in Britain around the end of the fifth century AD. In the following years they drove the native Britons back into remote areas of Wales and Cornwall, and established their own kingdoms. These grew in size to become large and powerful, such as the kingdoms of Mercia, Northumbria and Wessex. The Anglo-Saxons also brought and developed arts and culture, and, after becoming Christian, built many beautiful churches and monasteries. Later the various kingdoms united to become a single unit – England, or Angle-Land – with one king. The last Anglo-Saxon king of England was Harold I, who was defeated and killed at the Battle of Hastings by William of Normandy in 1066 AD. This defeat saw the end of the Anglo-Saxons as rulers of England, but their inheritance and influence is still with us. Most of our modern-day towns, for example, were originally built by the Anglo-Saxons, and have Anglo-Saxon names.

Using books, CD-ROMS and the internet, see what you can find out about the Anglo-Saxons, their history, and their culture.

Taking inspiration from Beowulf

Finally, here's a piece of writing by my daughter. She wrote it at school when she was in Year 7, as an exercise set by her English teacher when her class was studying the poem. I've included it here because I think it's a good example of how a poem over a thousand years old still has the power to inspire new work. Beowulf's fight with Grendel is described from the point of view of a young Scylding warrior.

> I saw the wisdom in his eyes, the strength in his soul and the courage in his heart. Beowulf.
> As the firelight danced upon the walls and the floor, and the shadows crept deeper into the tangled webs of the night, Hrothgar beckoned the young warrior to him. There was much talk, most of

LOOKING BACK AT THE PLAY

which I could not hear, but when a mighty cheer hit the carved ceiling of the great hall, I could do no more but to cheer and laugh with them. After the great feast had been held and the mead was drunk, and the horns were shallow and empty, I crept quietly out of my sleeping quarters. I wouldn't have dared do it alone, not without the mighty Beowulf to protect me from the night-stalker, the monster that writhed with evil and bubbled with hate. His hair tangled and torn, his flesh puckered and coiled, and his eyes, slit and awake with the sight of hunger.

No one could call him any name but Grendel.

I shivered as I lay down by the curling, thick ashes, hoping that what I saw would not be as gruesome or as horrible as I thought it would be. The fire which had once danced upon the walls was now dead, and was seeping into the wood and coal, twisting into a snake that slithered and slinked into the un-holy darkness.

Suddenly the doors burst open, and silver light poured into the great hall. Against a pale and fragile moon stood Grendel. His crumpled body swayed slightly as his eyes dashed around the room for his first victim.

He was chosen.

Reaching out an immense arm, he grabbed the fated warrior, and before the man had time to scream, Grendel swallowed him whole, letting the warm blood trickle down his chin and neck.

I shrank back into the shadows and looked at Beowulf, but he wasn't where he had been before. By the long bench of the hall he was struggling with the mighty Grendel himself. I pushed myself back even further, crouching in the fireplace and the dark. Chairs tumbled and tables splintered and cracked, swords on the walls and benches clanked and clinked as they were toppled to the ground. Beowulf never let his grip loosen or weaken. His hand and grip stayed true to the king and to his fellow men as he battled ferociously with the snarling and biting Grendel.

Suddenly, there was a crack and Grendel howled like a wolf to the silver-rocked moon, and, limping in agony and pain, he shuffled into the courtyard and out onto the plains, his sobs and cries echoing about the tallest mountains and moors.

The bloody arm was hung upon the wall. It was lit with the

LOOKING BACK AT THE PLAY

firelight of orange dancers prancing in the neatly-made hearth by the wall. I sat down next to Beowulf at the great table, examining the treasures that Hrothgar the King had given to Beowulf as a reward. Rubies and sapphires glistened in the glow of the flames, and golden coins and riches beyond any man's wildest dreams glinted and sparkled before my eyes. A golden staff lay, long and beautiful, on the outstretched table, with the head of a monkey and two blue gems for its staring eyes. Then we all sat on the wooden floor by the happy, crackling fire, and let Beowulf tell of his heroic fight with Grendel, and how he managed to rip off the monster's arm and send him limping into the lonely world outside.

"Take it!" he laughed, when I asked him of the golden monkey staff. "It will be of no use to me!"

So, thanking him again and again, I went to my quarters and looked out over the sleepy town, that was just stretching and awakening from its warm sleep. The red sun glinted over the houses, sending peace to the land and happiness to everyone's heart. It sent happiness to mine, and I felt even more so when I thought there would be no Grendel to haunt our halls, no black shadow seeping into the darkness at night, no death to come to any of our people. And I knew I owed my life and happiness to Beowulf.

Helen Calcutt